Workshop on Multiword Expressions: Identification, Interpretation, Disambiguation and Applications 2009

(MWE 2009)

Held at ACL-IJCNLP 2009

Singapore
6 August 2009

ISBN: 978-1-61738-450-9

Printed from e-media with permission by:

Curran Associates, Inc.
57 Morehouse Lane
Red Hook, NY 12571

Some format issues inherent in the e-media version may also appear in this print version.

Printed by Curran Associates, Inc. (2010)

Association for Computational Linguistics
209 N. Eighth Street
Stroudsburg, Pennsylvania 18360

Phone: 1-570-476-8006
Fax: 1-570-476-0860

acl@aclweb.org

Additional copies of this publication are available from:

Curran Associates, Inc.
57 Morehouse Lane
Red Hook, NY 12571 USA
Phone: 845-758-0400
Fax: 845-758-2634
Email: curran@proceedings.com
Web: www.proceedings.com

Introduction

The ACL 2009 Workshop on Multiword Expressions: Identification, Interpretation, Disambiguation and Applications (MWE'09) took place on August 6, 2009 in Singapore, immediately following the annual meeting of the Association for Computational Linguistics (ACL). This is the fifth time this workshop has been held in conjunction with ACL, following the meetings in 2003, 2004, 2006, and 2007.

The workshop focused on Multi-Word Expressions (MWEs), which represent an indispensable part of natural languages and appear steadily on a daily basis, both novel and already existing but paraphrased, which makes them important for many natural language applications. Unfortunately, while easily mastered by native speakers, MWEs are often non-compositional, which poses a major challenge for both foreign language learners and automatic analysis.

The growing interest in MWEs in the NLP community has led to many specialized workshops held every year since 2001 in conjunction with ACL, EACL and LREC; there have been also two recent special issues on MWEs published by leading journals: the International Journal of Language Resources and Evaluation, and the Journal of Computer Speech and Language.

As a result of the overall progress in the field, the time has come to move from basic preliminary research to actual applications in real-world NLP tasks. Thus, in MWE'09, we were interested in the overall process of dealing with MWEs, asking for original research on the following four fundamental topics:

Identification. Identifying MWEs in free text is a very challenging problem. Due to the variability of expression, it does not suffice to collect and use a static list of known MWEs; complex rules and machine learning are typically needed as well.

Interpretation. Semantically interpreting MWEs is a central issue. For some kinds of MWEs, e.g., noun compounds, it could mean specifying their semantics using a static inventory of semantic relations, e.g., WordNet-derived. In other cases, MWE's semantics could be expressible by a suitable paraphrase.

Disambiguation. Most MWEs are ambiguous in various ways. A typical disambiguation task is to determine whether an MWE is used non-compositionally (i.e., figuratively) or compositionally (i.e., literally) in a particular context.

Applications. Identifying MWEs in context and understanding their syntax and semantics is important for many natural language applications, including but not limited to question answering, machine translation, information retrieval, information extraction, and textual entailment. Still, despite the growing research interest, there are not enough successful applications in real NLP problems, which we believe is the key for the advancement of the field.

Of course, the above topics largely overlap. For example, identification can require disambiguating between literal and idiomatic uses since MWEs are typically required to be non-compositional by definition. Similarly, interpreting three-word noun compounds like *morning flight ticket* and *plastic water bottle* requires disambiguation between a left and a right syntactic structure, while interpreting two-word compounds like *English teacher* requires disambiguating between (a) 'teacher who teaches English' and (b) 'teacher coming from England (who could teach any subject, e.g., math)'.

We received 18 submissions, and, given our limited capacity as a one-day workshop, we were only able to accept 9 full papers for oral presentation, an acceptance rate of 50%.

We would like to thank the members of the Program Committee for their timely reviews. We would also like to thank the authors for their valuable contributions.

Dimitra Anastasiou, Chikara Hashimoto, Preslav Nakov, and Su Nam Kim
Co-Organizers

Organizers:

Dimitra Anastasiou, Localisation Research Centre, Limerick University, Ireland
Chikara Hashimoto, National Institute of Information and Communications Technology, Japan
Preslav Nakov, National University of Singapore, Singapore
Su Nam Kim, University of Melbourne, Australia

Program Committee:

Iñaki Alegria, University of the Basque Country (Spain)
Timothy Baldwin, University of Melbourne (Australia)
Colin Bannard, Max Planck Institute (Germany)
Francis Bond, National Institute of Information and Communications Technology (Japan)
Gaël Dias, Beira Interior University (Portugal)
Ulrich Heid, Stuttgart University (Germany)
Stefan Evert, University of Osnabrück (Germany)
Afsaneh Fazly, University of Toronto (Canada)
Nicole Grégoire, University of Utrecht (The Netherlands)
Roxana Girju, University of Illinois at Urbana-Champaign (USA)
Kyo Kageura, University of Tokyo (Japan)
Brigitte Krenn, Austrian Research Institute for Artificial Intelligence (Austria)
Éric Laporte, University of Marne-la-Vallée (France)
Rosamund Moon, University of Birmingham (UK)
Diana McCarthy, University of Sussex (UK)
Jan Odijk, University of Utrecht (The Netherlands)
Stephan Oepen, University of Oslo (Norway)
Darren Pearce, London Knowledge Lab (UK)
Pavel Pecina, Charles University (Czech Republic)
Scott Piao, University of Manchester (UK)
Violeta Seretan, University of Geneva (Switzerland)
Stan Szpakowicz, University of Ottawa (Canada)
Beata Trawinski, University of Tübingen (Germany)
Peter Turney, National Research Council of Canada (Canada)
Kiyoko Uchiyama, Keio University (Japan)
Begoña Villada Moirón, University of Groningen (The Netherlands)
Aline Villavicencio, Federal University of Rio Grande do Sul (Brazil)

Table of Contents

Workshop Program

Friday, August 6, 2009

8:30–8:45 Welcome and Introduction to the Workshop

Session 1 (08:45–10:00): MWE Identification and Disambiguation

08:45–09:10 *Statistically-Driven Alignment-Based Multiword Expression Identification for Technical Domains*
Helena Caseli, Aline Villavicencio, André Machado and Maria José Finatto

09:10–09:35 *Re-examining Automatic Keyphrase Extraction Approaches in Scientific Articles*
Su Nam Kim and Min-Yen Kan

09:35–10:00 *Verb Noun Construction MWE Token Classification*
Mona Diab and Pravin Bhutada

10:00-10:30 BREAK

Session 2 (10:30–12:10): Identification, Interpretation, and Disambiguation

10:30–10:55 *Exploiting Translational Correspondences for Pattern-Independent MWE Identification*
Sina Zarrieß and Jonas Kuhn

10:55–11:20 *A re-examination of lexical association measures*
Hung Huu Hoang, Su Nam Kim and Min-Yen Kan

11:20–11:45 *Mining Complex Predicates In Hindi Using A Parallel Hindi-English Corpus*
R. Mahesh K. Sinha

11:45-13:50 LUNCH

Session 3 (13:50–15:30): Applications

13:50–14:15 *Improving Statistical Machine Translation Using Domain Bilingual Multiword Expressions*
Zhixiang Ren, Yajuan Lü, Jie Cao, Qun Liu and Yun Huang

14:15–14:40 *Bottom-up Named Entity Recognition using Two-stage Machine Learning Method*
Hirotaka Funayama, Tomohide Shibata and Sadao Kurohashi

14:40–15:05 *Abbreviation Generation for Japanese Multi-Word Expressions*
Hiromi Wakaki, Hiroko Fujii, Masaru Suzuki, Mika Fukui and Kazuo Sumita

15:05-15:30 Discussion of Sessions 1, 2, 3 (Creating an Agenda for the general discussion)

15:30-16:00 BREAK

16:00-17:00 General Discussion

17:00-17:15 Closing Remarks

Statistically-Driven Alignment-Based Multiword Expression Identification for Technical Domains

Helena de Medeiros Caseli◇**, Aline Villavicencio**♣♠**, André Machado**♣**, Maria José Finatto**♡

◇Department of Computer Science, Federal University of São Carlos (Brazil)
♣Institute of Informatics, Federal University of Rio Grande do Sul (Brazil)
♠Department of Computer Sciences, Bath University (UK)
♡Institute of Language and Linguistics, Federal University of Rio Grande do Sul (Brazil)
helenacaseli@dc.ufscar.br, avillavicencio@inf.ufrgs.br,
ammachado@inf.ufrgs.br, mfinatto@terra.com.br

Abstract

Multiword Expressions (MWEs) are one of the stumbling blocks for more precise Natural Language Processing (NLP) systems. Particularly, the lack of coverage of MWEs in resources can impact negatively on the performance of tasks and applications, and can lead to loss of information or communication errors. This is especially problematic in technical domains, where a significant portion of the vocabulary is composed of MWEs. This paper investigates the use of a statistically-driven alignment-based approach to the identification of MWEs in technical corpora. We look at the use of several sources of data, including parallel corpora, using English and Portuguese data from a corpus of Pediatrics, and examining how a second language can provide relevant cues for this tasks. We report results obtained by a combination of statistical measures and linguistic information, and compare these to the reported in the literature. Such an approach to the (semi-)automatic identification of MWEs can considerably speed up lexicographic work, providing a more targeted list of MWE candidates.

1 Introduction

A multiword expression (MWE) can be defined as any word combination for which the syntactic or semantic properties of the whole expression cannot be obtained from its parts (Sag et al., 2002). Examples of MWEs are phrasal verbs (*break down, rely on*), compounds (*police car, coffee machine*), idioms (*rock the boat, let the cat out of the bag*). They are very numerous in languages, as Biber et al. (1999) note, accouting for between 30% and 45% of spoken English and 21% of academic prose, and for Jackendoff (1997) the number of MWEs in a speaker's lexicon is of the same order of magnitude as the number of single words. However, these estimates are likely to be underestimates if we consider that for language from a specific domain the specialized vocabulary is going to consist largely of MWEs (*global warming, protein sequencing*) and new MWEs are constantly appearing (*weapons of mass destruction, axis of evil*).

Multiword expressions play an important role in Natural Language Processing (NLP) applications, which should not only identify the MWEs but also be able to deal with them when they are found (Fazly and Stevenson, 2007). Failing to identify MWEs may cause serious problems for many NLP tasks, especially those envolving some kind of semantic processing. For parsing, for instance, Baldwin et al. (2004), found that for a random sample of 20,000 strings from the British National Corpus (BNC) even with a broad-coverage grammar for English (Flickinger, 2000) missing MWEs accounted for 8% of total parsing errors. Therefore, there is an enormous need for robust (semi-)automated ways of acquiring lexical information for MWEs (Villavicencio et al., 2007) that can significantly extend the coverage of resources. For example, one can more than double the number of verb-particle constructions (VPCs) entries in a dictionary, such as the Alvey Natural Language Tools (Carroll and Grover, 1989), just extracting VPCs from a corpus like the BNC (Baldwin, 2005). Furthermore, as MWEs are language dependent and culturally motivated, identifying the adequate translation of MWE occurrences is an important challenge for machine translation methods.

In this paper, we investigate experimentally the use of an alignment-based approach for the identification of MWEs in technical corpora. We look at the use of several sources of data, including par-

Proceedings of the 2009 Workshop on Multiword Expressions, ACL-IJCNLP 2009, pages 1–8,
Suntec, Singapore, 6 August 2009. ©2009 ACL and AFNLP

allel corpora, using English and Portuguese data from a corpus of Pediatrics, and examining how a second language can provide relevant cues for this tasks. In this way, cost-effective tools for the automatic alignment of texts can generate a list of MWE candidates with their appropriate translations. Such an approach to the (semi-)automatic identification of MWEs can considerably speed up lexicographic work, providing a more targeted list of MWE candidates and their translations, for the construction of bilingual resources, and/or with some semantic information for monolingual resources.

The remainder of this paper is structured as follows. Section 2 briefly discusses MWEs and some previous works on methods for automatically extracting them. Section 3 presents the resources used while section 4 describes the methods proposed to extract MWEs as a statistically-driven by-product of an automatic word alignment process. Section 5 presents the evaluation methodology and analyses the results and section 6 finishes this paper with some conclusions and proposals for future work.

2 Related Work

The term Multiword Expression has been used to describe a large number of distinct but related phenomena, such as phrasal verbs (e.g. *come along*), nominal compounds (e.g. *frying pan*), institutionalised phrases (e.g. *bread and butter*), and many others (Sag et al., 2002). They are very frequent in everyday language and this is reflected in several existing grammars and lexical resources, where almost half of the entries are Multiword Expressions.

However, due to their heterogeneous characteristics, MWEs present a tough challenge for both linguistic and computational work (Sag et al., 2002). Some MWEs are fixed, and do not present internal variation, such as *ad hoc*, while others allow different degrees of internal variability and modification, such as *touch a nerve* (*touch/find a nerve*) and *spill beans* (*spill several/musical/mountains of beans*). In terms of semantics, some MWEs are more opaque in their meaning (e.g. *to kick the bucket* as *to die*), while others have more transparent meanings that can be inferred from the words in the MWE (e.g. *eat up*, where the particle *up* adds a completive sense to *eat*). Therefore, providing appropriate methods for the automatic identification and treatment of these phenomena is a real challenge for NLP systems.

A variety of approaches has been proposed for automatically identifying MWEs, differing basically in terms of the type of MWE and language to which they apply, and the sources of information they use. Although some work on MWEs is type independent (e.g. (Zhang et al., 2006; Villavicencio et al., 2007)), given the heterogeneity of MWEs much of the work looks instead at specific types of MWE like collocations (Pearce, 2002), compounds (Keller and Lapata, 2003) and VPCs (Baldwin, 2005; Villavicencio, 2005; Carlos Ramisch and Aline Villavicencio and Leonardo Moura and Marco Idiart, 2008). Some of these works concentrate on particular languages (e.g. (Pearce, 2002; Baldwin, 2005) for English and (Piao et al., 2006) for Chinese), but some work has also benefitted from asymmetries in languages, using information from one language to help deal with MWEs in the other (e.g. (na Villada Moirón and Tiedemann, 2006; Caseli et al., 2009)).

As basis for helping to determine whether a given sequence of words is in fact an MWE (e.g. *ad hoc* vs *the small boy*) some of these works employ linguistic knowledge for the task (Villavicencio, 2005), while others employ statistical methods (Pearce, 2002; Evert and Krenn, 2005; Zhang et al., 2006; Villavicencio et al., 2007) or combine them with some kinds of linguistic information such as syntactic and semantic properties (Baldwin and Villavicencio, 2002; Van de Cruys and na Villada Moirón, 2007) or automatic word alignment (na Villada Moirón and Tiedemann, 2006).

Statistical measures of association have been commonly used for this task, as they can be democratically applied to any language and MWE type. However, there is no consensus about which measure is best suited for identifying MWEs in general. Villavicencio et al. (2007) compared some of these measures (mutual information, permutation entropy and χ^2) for the type-independent detection of MWEs and found that Mutual Information seemed to differentiate MWEs from non-MWEs, but the same was not true of χ_2. In addition, Evert and Krenn (2005) found that for MWE identification the efficacy of a given measure depends on factors like the type of MWEs being targeted for identification, the domain and size of the corpora used, and the amount of low-frequency data excluded by adopting a threshold. Nonetheless, Villavicencio et al. (2007), discussing the influence of the corpus size and nature over the methods, found that these different measures have a high level of agreement about MWEs, whether in carefully constructed corpora or in more heterogeneous web-based ones. They also discuss the results obtained from adopting approaches like these for extending the coverage of resources, arguing that grammar coverage can be significantly increased if MWEs are properly identified and treated (Villavicencio et al., 2007).

Among the methods that use additional information along with statistics to extract MWE, the one proposed by na Villada Moirón and Tiedemann (2006) seems to be the most similar to our approach. The main difference between them is the way in which word alignment is used in the MWE extraction process. In this paper, the word alignment is the basis for the MWE extraction process while Villada Moirón and Tiedemann's method uses the alignment just for ranking the MWE candidates which were extracted on the basis of association measures (log-likelihood and salience) and head dependence heuristic (in parsed data).

Our approach, as described in details by Caseli et al. (2009), also follows to some extent that of Zhang et al. (2006), as missing lexical entries for MWEs and related constructions are detected via error mining methods, and this paper focuses on the extraction of generic MWEs as a by-product of an automatic word alignment. Another related work is the automatic detection of non-compositional compounds (NCC) by Melamed (1997) in which NCCs are identified by analyzing statistical translation models trained in a huge corpus by a time-demanding process.

Given this context, our approach proposes the use of alignment techniques for identifying MWEs, looking at sequences detected by the aligner as containing more than one word, which form the MWE candidates. As a result, sequences of two or more consecutive source words are treated as MWE candidates regardless of whether they are translated as one or more target words.

3 The Corpus and Reference Lists

The Corpus of Pediatrics used in these experiments contains 283 texts in Portuguese with a total of 785,448 words, extracted from the *Jornal de Pediatria*. From this corpus, the Pediatrics Glossary, a reference list containing multiword terms and recurring expressions, was semi-automatically constructed, and manually checked.[1] The primary aim of the Pediatrics Glossary, as an online resource for long-distance education, was to train, qualify and support translation students on the domain of pediatrics texts.

The Pediatrics Glossary was built from the 36,741 ngrams that occurred at least 5 times in the corpus. These were automatically cleaned or removed using some POS tag patterns (e.g. removing prepositions from terms that began or ended with them). In addition, if an ngram was part of a larger ngram, only the latter appeared in the Glossary, as is the case of *aleitamento materno* (*maternal breastfeeding*) which is excluded as it is contained in *aleitamento materno exclusivo* (*exclusive maternal breastfeeding*). This post-processing resulted in 3,645 ngrams, which were manually checked by translation students, and resulted in 2,407 terms, with 1,421 bigrams, 730 trigrams and 339 ngrams with n larger than 3 (not considered in the experiments presented in this paper).

4 Statistically-Driven and Alignment-Based methods

4.1 Statistically-Driven method

Statistical measures of association have been widely employed in the identification of MWEs. The idea behind their use is that they are an inexpensive language and type independent means of detecting recurrent patterns. As Firth famously said *a word is characterized by the company it keeps* and since we expect the component words of an MWE to occur frequently together, then these measures can give an indication of MWEness. In this way, if a group of words co-occurs with significantly high frequency when compared to the frequencies of the individual words, then they may form an MWE. Indeed, measures such as Pointwise Mutual Information (PMI), Mutual Information (MI), χ_2, log-likelihood (Press et al., 1992) and others have been employed for this task, and some of them seem to provide more accurate predictions of MWEness than others. In fact, in a comparison of some measures for the type-independent detection of MWEs, MI seemed

[1]Available in the TEXTQUIM/UFRGS website: `http://www.ufrgs.br/textquim`

to differentiate MWEs from non-MWEs, but the same was not true of χ_2 (Villavicencio et al., 2007). In this work we use two commonly employed measures for this task: PMI and MI, as implemented in the Ngram Statistics Package (Banerjee and Pedersen, 2003).

From the Portuguese portion of the Corpus of Pediatrics, 196,105 bigram and 362,663 trigram MWE candidates were generated, after filtering ngrams containing punctuation and numbers. In order to evaluate how these methods perform without any linguistic filtering, the only threshold employed was a frequency cut-off of 2 occurrences, resulting in 64,839 bigrams and 54,548 trigrams. Each of the four measures were then calculated for these ngrams, and we ranked each n-gram according to each of these measures. The average of all the rankings is used as the combined measure of the MWE candidates.

4.2 Alignment-Based method

The second of the MWE extraction approaches to be investigated in this paper is the alignment-based method. The automatic word alignment of two parallel texts — a text written in one (source) language and its translation to another (target) language — is the process of searching for correspondences between source and target words and sequences of words. For each word in a source sentence equivalences in the parallel target sentence are looked for. Therefore, taking into account a word alignment between a source word sequence S ($S = s_1 \ldots s_n$ with $n \geq 2$) and a target word sequence T ($T = t_1 \ldots t_m$ with $m \geq 1$), that is $S \leftrightarrow T$, the alignmet-based MWE extracion method assumes that: (a) S and T share some semantic features, and (b) S may be a MWE.

In other words, the alignment-based MWE extraction method states that the sequence S will be a MWE candidate if it is aligned with a sequence T composed of one or more words (a $n : m$ alignment with $n \geq 2$ and $m \geq 1$). For example, the sequence of two Portuguese words *aleitamento materno* — which occurs 202 times in the corpus used in our experiments — is a MWE candidate because these two words were joined to be aligned 184 times with the word *breastfeeding* (a $2 : 1$ alignment), 8 times with the word *breastfed* (a $2 : 1$ alignment), 2 times with *breastfeeding practice* (a $2 : 2$ alignment) and so on.

Thus, notice that the alignment-based MWE extraction method does not rely on the conceptual asymmetries between languages since it does not expect that a source sequence of words be aligned with a single target word. The method looks for the sequences of source words that are frequently joined together during the alignment despite the number of target words involved. These features indicate that the method priorizes precision in spite of recall.

It is also important to say that although the sequences of source and target words resemble the phrases used in the phrase-based statistical machine translation (SMT), they are indeed a refinement of them. More specifically, although both approaches rely on word alignments performed by `GIZA++`[2] (Och and Ney, 2000), in the alignment-based approach not all sequences of words are considered as phrases (and MWE candidates) but just those with an alignment $n : m$ ($n >= 2$) with a target sequence. To confirm this assumption a phrase-based SMT system was trained with the same corpus used in our experiments and the number of phrases extracted following both approaches were compared. While the SMT extracted 819,208 source phrases, our alignment-based approach (without applying any part-of-speech or frequency filter) extracted only 34,277. These results show that the alignment-based approach refines in some way the phrases of SMT systems.

In this paper, we investigate experimentally whether MWEs can be identified as a by-product of the automatic word alignment of parallel texts. We focus on Portuguese MWEs from the Corpus of Pediatrics and the evaluation is performed using the bigrams and trigrams from the Pediatrics Glossary as gold standard.

To perform the extraction of MWE candidates following the alignment-based approach, first, the original corpus had to be sentence and word aligned and Part-of-Speech (POS) tagged. For these preprocessing steps were used, respectively: a version of the Translation Corpus Aligner (TCA) (Hofland, 1996), the statistical word aligner `GIZA++` (Och and Ney, 2000) and the morphological analysers and POS taggers from `Apertium`[3] (Armentano-Oller et al., 2006).

[2] `GIZA++` is a well-known statistical word aligner that can be found at: `http://www.fjoch.com/GIZA++.html`

[3] `Apertium` is an open-source machine translation engine and toolbox available at: `http://www.apertium.org`.

From the preprocessed corpus, the MWE candidates are extracted as those in which two or more words have the same alignment, that is, they are linked to the same target unit. This initial list of MWE candidates is, then, filtered to remove those candidates that: (a) match some sequences of POS tags or words (patterns) defined in previous experiments (Caseli et al., 2009) or (b) whose frequency is below a certain threshold. The remaining units in the candidate list are considered to be MWEs.

Several filtering patterns and minimum frequency thresholds were tested and three of them are presented in details here. The first one (F1) is the same used during the manual building of the reference lists of MWEs: (a) patterns beginning with Article + Noun and beginning or finishing with verbs and (b) with a minimum frequency threshold of 5.

The second one (F2) is the same used in the (Caseli et al., 2009), mainly: (a) patterns beginning with determiner, auxiliary verb, pronoun, adverb, conjunction and surface forms such as those of the verb *to be* (*are*, *is*, *was*, *were*), relatives (*that*, *what*, *when*, *which*, *who*, *why*) and prepositions (*from*, *to*, *of*) and (b) with a minimum frequency threshold of 2.

And the third one (F3) is the same as (Caseli et al., 2009) plus: (a) patterns beginning or finishing with determiner, adverb, conjunction, preposition, verb, pronoun and numeral and (b) with a minimum frequency threshold of 2.

5 Experiments and Results

Table 1 shows the top 5 and the bottom 5 ranked candidates returned by PMI and the alignment-based approach. Although some of the results are good, especially the top candidates, there is still considerable noise among the candidates, as for instance *jogar video game* (lit. *play video game*). From table 1 it is also possible to notice that the alignment-based approach indeed extracts Pediatrics terms such as *aleitamento materno* (*breast-feeding*) and also other possible MWE that are not Pediatrics terms such as *estados unidos* (*United States*).

In table 2 we show the precision (number of correct candidates among the proposed ones), recall (number of correct candidates among those in reference lists) and F-measure ($(2 * precision * recall)/(precision + recall)$) figures for the association measures using all the candidates (on the first half of the table) and using the top 1,421 bigram and 730 trigram candidates (on the second half). From these latter results, we can see that the top candidates produced by these measures do not agree with the Pediatrics Glossary, since there are only at most 18.37% bigram and 6.03% trigram MWEs among the top candidates, as ranked by MI and PMI respectively. Interestingly, MI had a better performance for bigrams while for trigrams PMI performed better.

PMI	**alignment-based**
Online Mendelian Inheritance	faixa etária
Beta Technology Incorporated	aleitamento materno
Lange Beta Technology	estados unidos
Oxido Nitrico Inalatorio	hipertensão arterial
jogar video game	leite materno
...	...
e um de	couro cabeludo
e a do	bloqueio lactíferos
se que de	emocional anatomia
e a da	neonato a termo
e de nao	duplas mães bebês

Table 1: Top 5 and Bottom 5 MWE candidates ranked by PMI and alignment-based approach

pt MWE candidates	**PMI**	**MI**
# proposed bigrams	64,839	64,839
# correct MWEs	1403	1403
precision	2.16%	2.16%
recall	98.73%	98.73%
F	4.23%	4.23%
# proposed trigrams	54,548	54,548
# correct MWEs	701	701
precision	1.29%	1.29%
recall	96.03%	96.03%
F	2.55%	2.55%
# proposed bigrams	1,421	1,421
# correct MWEs	155	261
precision	10.91%	18.37%
recall	10.91%	18.37%
F	10.91%	18.37%
# proposed trigrams	730	730
# correct MWEs	44	20
precision	6.03%	2.74%
recall	6.03%	2.74%
F	6.03%	2.74%

Table 2: Evaluation of MWE candidates - PMI and MI

On the other hand, looking at the alignment-based method, 34,277 pt MWE candidates were extracted and Table 3 sumarizes the number of candidates filtered following the three filters described in 4.2: F1, F2 and F3.

To evaluate the efficacy of the alignment-based method in identifying multiword terms of Pediatrics, an automatic comparison was performed using the Pediatrics Glossary. In this auto-

pt MWE candidates	F1	F2	F3
# filtered by POS patterns	24,996	21,544	32,644
# filtered by frequency	9,012	11,855	1,442
# final Set	269	878	191

Table 3: Number of pt MWE candidates filtered in the alignment-based approach

pt MWE candidates	F1	F2	F3
# proposed bigrams	250	754	169
# correct MWEs	48	95	65
precision	19.20%	12.60%	38.46%
recall	3.38%	6.69%	4.57%
F	5.75%	8.74%	8.18%
# proposed trigrams	19	110	20
# correct MWEs	1	9	4
precision	5.26%	8.18%	20.00%
recall	0.14%	1.23%	0.55%
F	0.27%	2.14%	1.07%
# proposed bi/trigrams	269	864	189
# correct MWEs	49	104	69
precision	18.22%	12.04%	36,51%
recall	2.28%	4.83%	3.21%
F	4.05%	6.90%	5.90%

Table 4: Evaluation of MWE candidates

matic comparision we considered the final lists of MWEs candidates generated by each filter in table 3. The number of matching entries and the values for precision, recall and F-measure are showed in table 4.

The different values of extracted MWEs (in table 3) and evaluated ones (in table 4) are due to the restriction of considering only bigrams and trigrams in the Pediatrics Glossary. Then, longer MWEs — such as *doença arterial coronariana prematura* (*premature coronary artery disease*) and *pequenos para idade gestacional* (*small for gestational age*) — extracted by the alignment-based method are not being considered at the moment.

After the automatic comparison using the Pediatrics Glossary, an analysis by human experts was performed on one of the derived lists — that with the best precision values so far (from filter F3). The human analysis was necessary since, as stated in (Caseli et al., 2009), the coverage of reference lists may be low, and it is likely that a lot of MWE candidates that were not found in the Pediatrics Glossary are nonetheless true MWEs. In this paper only the pt MWE candidates extracted using filter F3 (as described in section 4.2) were manually evaluated.

From the 191 pt MWE candidates extracted after F3, 69 candidates (36.1% of the total amount) were found in the bigrams or trigrams in the Glossary (see table 4). Then, the remaining 122 candidates (63.9%) were analysed by two native-speakers human judges, who classified each of the 122 candidates as true, if it is a multiword expression, or false, otherwise independently of being a Pediatrics term. For the judges, a sequence of words was considered a MWE mainly if it was: (1) a proper name or (2) a sequence of words for which the meaning cannot be obtained by compounding the meanings of its component words.

The judgments of both judges were compared and a disagreement of approximately 12% on multiwords was verified. This disagreement was also measured by the kappa (K) measure (Carletta, 1996), with $k = 0.73$, which does not prevent conclusions to be drawn. According to Carletta (1996), among other authors, a value of k between 0.67 and 0.8 indicates a good agreement.

In order to calculate the percentage of true candidates among the 122, two approaches can be followed, depending on what criteria one wants to emphasize: precision or coverage (not recall because we are not calculating regarding a reference list). To emphasize the precision, one should consider as genuine MWEs only those candidates classified as true by both judges, on the other hand, to emphasize the coverage, one should consider also those candidates classified as true by just one of them. So, from 191 MWE candidates, 126 (65.97%) were classified as true by both judges and 145 (75.92%) by at least one of them.

6 Conclusions and Future Work

MWEs are a complex and heterogeneous set of phenomena that defy attempts to capture them fully, but due to their role in communication they need to be properly accounted for in NLP applications and tasks.

In this paper we investigated the identification of MWEs from technical domain, testing statistically-driven and alignment-based approaches for identifying MWEs from a Pediatrics parallel corpus. The alignment-based method generates a targeted precision-oriented list of MWE candidates, while the statistical methods produce recall-oriented results at the expense of precision. Therefore, the combination of these methods can produce a set of MWE candidates that is both more precise than the latter and has more coverage than the former. This can significantly speed up lexicographic work. Moreover, the results obtained show that in comparison with the manual extraction of MWEs, this approach can provide also a general set of MWE candidates in addition to the manually selected technical terms.

Using the alignment-based extraction method we notice that it is possible to extract MWEs that are Pediatrics terms with a precision of 38% for bigrams and 20% for trigrams, but with very low recall since only the MWEs in the Pediatrics Glossary were considered correct. However, after a manual analysis carried out by two native speakers of Portuguese we found that the percentage of true MWEs considered by both or at least one of them were, respectively, 65.97% and 75.92%. This was a significative improvement but it is important to say that, in this manual analysis, the human experts classified the MWEs as true independently of them being Pediatrics terms. So, as future work we intend to carry out a more carefull analysis with experts in Pediatrics to evaluate how many MWEs candidates are also Pediatrics terms.

In addition, we plan to investigate a weighted combination of these methods, favouring those that have better precision. Finally, we also intend to apply the results obtained in to the semi-automatic construction of ontologies.

Acknowledgments

We would like to thank the TEXTQUIM/UFRGS group for making the Corpus of Pediatrics and Pediatrics Glossary available to us. We also thank the financial support of FAPESP in bulding the parallel corpus. This research has been partly funded by the FINEP project COMUNICA.

References

Carme Armentano-Oller, Rafael C. Carrasco, Antonio M. Corbí-Bellot, Mikel L. Forcada, Mireia Ginestí-Rosell, Sergio Ortiz-Rojas, Juan Antonio Pérez-Ortiz, Gema Ramírez-Sánchez, Felipe Sánchez-Martínez, and Miriam A. Scalco. 2006. Open-source Portuguese-Spanish machine translation. In R. Vieira, P. Quaresma, M.G.V. Nunes, N.J. Mamede, C. Oliveira, and M.C. Dias, editors, *Proceedings of the 7th International Workshop on Computational Processing of Written and Spoken Portuguese, (PROPOR 2006)*, volume 3960 of *Lecture Notes in Computer Science*, pages 50–59. Springer-Verlag, May.

Timothy Baldwin and Aline Villavicencio. 2002. Extracting the Unextractable: A Case Study on Verb-particles. In *Proceedings of the 6th Conference on Natural Language Learning (CoNLL-2002)*, pages 98–104, Taipei, Taiwan.

Timothy Baldwin, Emily M. Bender, Dan Flickinger, Ara Kim, and Stephan Oepen. 2004. Road-testing the English Resource Grammar over the British National Corpus. In *Proceedings of the Fourth International Conference on Language Resources and Evaluation (LREC 2004)*, pages 2047–2050, Lisbon, Portugal.

Timothy Baldwin. 2005. The deep lexical acquisition of English verb-particles. *Computer Speech and Language, Special Issue on Multiword Expressions*, 19(4):398–414.

Satanjeev Banerjee and Ted Pedersen. 2003. The Design, Implementation and Use of the Ngram Statistics Package. In *In Proceedings of the Fourth International Conference on Intelligent Text Processing and Computational Linguistics*, pages 370–381.

Douglas Biber, Stig Johansson, Geoffrey Leech, Susan Conrad, and Edward Finegan. 1999. *Grammar of Spoken and Written English*. Longman, Harlow.

Jean Carletta. 1996. Assessing agreement on classification tasks: the kappa statistics. *Computational Linguistics*, 22(2):249–254.

Carlos Ramisch and Aline Villavicencio and Leonardo Moura and Marco Idiart. 2008. Picking them up and Figuring them out: Verb-Particle Constructions, Noise and Idiomaticity. In *Proceedings of the 12th Conference on Computational Natural Language Learning (CoNLL 2008)*, pages 49–56.

John Carroll and Claire Grover. 1989. The derivation of a large computational lexicon of English from LDOCE. In Bran Boguraev and Ted Briscoe, editors, *Computational Lexicography for Natural Language Processing*, pages 117–134. Longman, Harlow, UK.

Helena M. Caseli, Carlos Ramisch, Maria G. V. Nunes, and Aline Villavicencio. 2009. Alignment-based extraction of multiword expressions. *Language Resources and Evaluation*, to appear.

Stefan Evert and Brigitte Krenn. 2005. Using small random samples for the manual evaluation of statistical association measures. *Computer Speech and Language*, 19(4):450–466.

Afsaneh Fazly and Suzanne Stevenson. 2007. Distinguishing Subtypes of Multiword Expressions Using Linguistically-Motivated Statistical Measures. In *Proceedings of the Workshop on A Broader Perspective on Multiword Expressions*, pages 9–16, Prague, June.

Dan Flickinger. 2000. On building a more efficient grammar by exploiting types. *Natural Language Engineering*, 6(1):15–28.

Knut Hofland. 1996. A program for aligning English and Norwegian sentences. In S. Hockey, N. Ide, and G. Perissinotto, editors, *Research in Humanities Computing*, pages 165–178, Oxford. Oxford University Press.

Ray Jackendoff. 1997. Twistin' the night away. *Language*, 73:534–59.

Frank Keller and Mirella Lapata. 2003. Using the Web to Obtain Frequencies for Unseen Bigrams. *Computational Linguistics*, 29(3):459–484.

I. Dan Melamed. 1997. Automatic Discovery of Non-Compositional Compounds in Parallel Data. In *eprint arXiv:cmp-lg/9706027*, pages 6027–+, June.

Bego na Villada Moirón and Jorg Tiedemann. 2006. Identifying idiomatic expressions using automatic word-alignment. In *Proceedings of the Workshop on Multi-word-expressions in a Multilingual Context (EACL-2006)*, pages 33–40, Trento, Italy.

Franz Josef Och and Hermann Ney. 2000. Improved statistical alignment models. In *Proceedings of the 38th Annual Meeting of the ACL*, pages 440–447, Hong Kong, China, October.

Darren Pearce. 2002. A Comparative Evaluation of Collocation Extraction Techniques. In *Proceedings of the Third International Conference on Language Resources and Evaluation*, pages 1–7, Las Palmas, Canary Islands, Spain.

Scott S. L. Piao, Guangfan Sun, Paul Rayson, and Qi Yuan. 2006. Automatic Extraction of Chinese Multiword Expressions with a Statistical Tool. In *Proceedings of the Workshop on Multi-word-expressions in a Multilingual Context (EACL-2006)*, pages 17–24, Trento, Italy, April.

William H. Press, Saul A. Teukolsky, William T. Vetterling, and Brian P. Flannery. 1992. *Numerical Recipes in C: The Art of Scientific Computing. Second edition.* Cambridge University Press.

Ivan A. Sag, Timothy Baldwin, Francis Bond, Ann Copestake, and Dan Flickinger. 2002. Multiword Expressions: A Pain in the Neck for NLP. In *Proceedings of the Third International Conference on Computational Linguistics and Intelligent Text Processing (CICLing-2002)*, volume 2276 of *(Lecture Notes in Computer Science)*, pages 1–15, London, UK. Springer-Verlag.

Tim Van de Cruys and Bego na Villada Moirón. 2007. Semantics-based Multiword Expression Extraction. In *Proceedings of the Workshop on A Broader Prespective on Multiword Expressions*, pages 25–32, Prague, June.

Aline Villavicencio, Valia Kordoni, Yi Zhang, Marco Idiart, and Carlos Ramisch. 2007. Validation and Evaluation of Automatically Acquired Multiword Expressions for Grammar Engineering. In *Proceedings of the 2007 Joint Conference on Empirical Methods in Natural Language Processing and Computational Natural Language Learning*, pages 1034–1043, Prague, June.

Aline Villavicencio. 2005. The Availability of Verb-Particle Constructions in Lexical Resources: How Much is Enough? *Journal of Computer Speech and Language Processing*, 19(4):415–432.

Yi Zhang, Valia Kordoni, Aline Villavicencio, and Marco Idiart. 2006. Automated Multiword Expression Prediction for Grammar Engineering. In *Proceedings of the Workshop on Multiword Expressions: Identifying and Exploiting Underlying Properties*, pages 36–44, Sydney, Australia, July. Association for Computational Linguistics.

Re-examining Automatic Keyphrase Extraction Approaches in Scientific Articles

Su Nam Kim
CSSE dept.
University of Melbourne
snkim@csse.unimelb.edu.au

Min-Yen Kan
Department of Computer Science
National University of Singapore
kanmy@comp.nus.edu.sg

Abstract

We tackle two major issues in automatic keyphrase extraction using scientific articles: *candidate selection* and *feature engineering*. To develop an efficient candidate selection method, we analyze the nature and variation of keyphrases and then select candidates using regular expressions. Secondly, we re-examine the existing features broadly used for the supervised approach, exploring different ways to enhance their performance. While most other approaches are supervised, we also study the optimal features for unsupervised keyphrase extraction. Our research has shown that effective candidate selection leads to better performance as evaluation accounts for candidate coverage. Our work also attests that many of existing features are also usable in unsupervised extraction.

1 Introduction

Keyphrases are simplex nouns or noun phrases (NPs) that represent the key ideas of the document. Keyphrases can serve as a representative summary of the document and also serve as high quality index terms. It is thus no surprise that keyphrases have been utilized to acquire critical information as well as to improve the quality of natural language processing (NLP) applications such as document summarizer(Dávanzo and Magnini, 2005), information retrieval (IR)(Gutwin et al., 1999) and document clustering(Hammouda et al., 2005).

In the past, various attempts have been made to boost automatic keyphrase extraction performance based primarily on statistics(Frank et al., 1999; Turney, 2003; Park et al., 2004; Wan and Xiao, 2008) and a rich set of heuristic features(Barker and Corrnacchia, 2000; Medelyan and Witten, 2006; Nguyen and Kan, 2007). In Section 2, we give a more comprehensive overview of previous attempts.

Current keyphrase technology still has much room for improvement. First of all, although several candidate selection methods have been proposed for automatic keyphrase extraction in the past (e.g. (Frank et al., 1999; Park et al., 2004; Nguyen and Kan, 2007)), most of them do not effectively deal with various keyphrase forms which results in the ignorance of some keyphrases as candidates. Moreover, no studies thus far have done a detailed investigation of the nature and variation of manually-provided keyphrases. As a consequence, the community lacks a standardized list of candidate forms, which leads to difficulties in direct comparison across techniques during evaluation and hinders re-usability.

Secondly, previous studies have shown the effectiveness of their own features but not many compared their features with other existing features. That leads to a redundancy in studies and hinders direct comparison. In addition, existing features are specifically designed for supervised approaches with few exceptions. However, this approach involves a large amount of manual labor, thus reducing its utility for real-world application. Hence, unsupervised approach is inevitable in order to minimize manual tasks and to encourage utilization. It is a worthy study to attest the reliability and re-usability for the unsupervised approach in order to set up the tentative guideline for applications.

This paper targets to resolve these issues of candidate selection and feature engineering. In our work on candidate selection, we analyze the nature and variation of keyphrases with the purpose of proposing a candidate selection method which improves the coverage of candidates that occur in various forms. Our second contribution re-examines existing keyphrase extraction features

Proceedings of the 2009 Workshop on Multiword Expressions, ACL-IJCNLP 2009, pages 9–16,
Suntec, Singapore, 6 August 2009.

reported in the literature, in terms of their effectiveness and re-usability. We test and compare the usefulness of each feature for further improvement. In addition, we assess how well these features can be applied in an unsupervised approach.

In the remaining sections, we describe an overview of related work in Section 2, our proposals on candidate selection and feature engineering in Section 4 and 5, our system architecture and data in Section 6. Then, we evaluate our proposals, discuss outcomes and conclude our work in Section 7, 8 and 9, respectively.

2 Related Work

The majority of related work has been carried out using statistical approaches, a rich set of symbolic resources and linguistically-motivated heuristics(Frank et al., 1999; Turney, 1999; Barker and Corrnacchia, 2000; Matsuo and Ishizuka, 2004; Nguyen and Kan, 2007). Features used can be categorized into three broad groups: (1) document cohesion features (i.e. relationship between document and keyphrases)(Frank et al., 1999; Matsuo and Ishizuka, 2004; Medelyan and Witten, 2006; Nguyen and Kan, 2007), and to lesser, (2) keyphrase cohesion features (i.e. relationship among keyphrases)(Turney, 2003) and (3) term cohesion features (i.e. relationship among components in a keyphrase)(Park et al., 2004).

The simplest system is `KEA` (Frank et al., 1999; Witten et al., 1999) that uses *TF*IDF* (i.e. term frequency * inverse document frequency) and first occurrence in the document. *TF*IDF* measures the document cohesion and the first occurrence implies the importance of the abstract or introduction which indicates the keyphrases have a locality. Turney (2003) added the notion of keyphrase cohesion to `KEA` features and Nguyen and Kan (2007) added linguistic features such as section information and suffix sequence. The `GenEx` system(Turney, 1999) employed an inventory of nine syntactic features, such as length in words and frequency of stemming phrase as a set of parametrized heuristic rules. Barker and Corrnacchia (2000) introduced a method based on head noun heuristics that took three features: length of candidate, frequency and head noun frequency. To take advantage of domain knowledge, Hulth et al. (2001) used a hierarchically-organized domain-specific thesaurus from Swedish Parliament as a secondary knowledge source. The `Textract` (Park et al., 2004) also ranks the candidate keyphrases by its judgment of keyphrases' degree of domain specificity based on subject-specific collocations(Damerau, 1993), in addition to term cohesion using Dice coefficient(Dice, 1945). Recently, Wan and Xiao (2008) extracts automatic keyphrases from single documents, utilizing document clustering information. The assumption behind this work is that the documents with the same or similar topics interact with each other in terms of salience of words. The authors first clustered the documents then used the graph-based ranking algorithm to rank the candidates in a document by making use of mutual influences of other documents in the same cluster.

3 Keyphrase Analysis

In previous study, `KEA` employed the indexing words as candidates whereas others such as (Park et al., 2004; Nguyen and Kan, 2007) generated handcrafted regular expression rules. However, none carefully undertook the analysis of keyphrases. We believe there is more to be learned from the reference keyphrases themselves by doing a fine-grained, careful analysis of their form and composition. Note that we used the articles collected from ACM digital library for both analyzing keyphrases as well as evaluating methods. See Section 6 for data in detail.

Syntactically, keyphrases can be formed by either simplex nouns (e.g. *algorithm, keyphrase, multi-agent*) or noun phrases (NPs) which can be a sequence of nouns and their auxiliary words such as adjectives and adverbs (e.g. *mobile network, fast computing, partially observable Markov decision process*) despite few incidences. They can also incorporate a prepositional phrase (PP) (e.g. *quality of service, policy of distributed caching*). When keyphrases take the form of an NP with an attached PP (i.e. NPs in *of-PP form*), the preposition *of* is most common, but others such as *for, in, via* also occur (e.g. *incentive <u>for</u> cooperation, inequality <u>in</u> welfare, agent security <u>via</u> approximate policy, trade <u>in</u> financial instrument <u>based on</u> logical formula*). The patterns above correlate well to part-of-speech (POS) patterns used in modern keyphrase extraction systems.

However, our analysis uncovered additional linguistic patterns and alternations which other studies may have overlooked. In our study we also found that keyphrases also occur as a simple con-

Criteria	Rules
Frequency	(**Rule1**) *Frequency heuristic* i.e. frequency ≥ 2 for simplex words vs. frequency ≥ 1 for NPs
Length	(**Rule2**) *Length heuristic* i.e. up to length 3 for NPs in non-*of-PP form* vs. up to length 4 for NPs in *of-PP form* (e.g. *synchronous concurrent program vs. model of multiagent interaction*)
Alternation	(**Rule3**) *of-PP form alternation* (e.g. *number of sensor = sensor number, history of past encounter = past encounter history*) (**Rule4**) *Possessive alternation* (e.g. *agent's goal = goal of agent, security's value = value of security*)
Extraction	(**Rule5**) *Noun Phrase* = $(NN\|NNS\|NNP\|NNPS\|JJ\|JJR\|JJS)^{*}(NN\|NNS\|NNP\|NNPS)$ (e.g. *complexity, effective algorithm, grid computing, distributed web-service discovery architecture*) (**Rule6**) *Simplex Word/NP IN Simplex Word/NP* (e.g. *quality of service, sensitivity of VOIP traffic (**VOIP traffic** extracted), simplified instantiation of zebroid (**simplified instantiation** extracted)*)

Table 1: Candidate Selection Rules

junctions (e.g. *search and rescue, propagation and delivery*), and much more rarely, as conjunctions of more complex NPs (e.g. *history of past encounter and transitivity*). Some keyphrases appear to be more complex (e.g. *pervasive document edit and management system, task and resource allocation in agent system*). Similarly, abbreviations and possessive forms figure as common patterns (e.g. *belief desire intention = BDI, inverse document frequency = (IDF); Bayes' theorem, agent's dominant strategy*).

A critical insight of our work is that keyphrases can be morphologically and semantically altered. Keyphrases that incorporate a PP or have an underlying genitive composition are often easily varied by word order alternation. Previous studies have used the altered keyphrases when forming in *of-PP form*. For example, *quality of service* can be altered to *service quality*, sometimes with little semantic difference. Also, as most morphological variation in English relates to noun number and verb inflection, keyphrases are subject to these rules as well (e.g. *distributed system* $\neq$ *distributing system, dynamical caching* $\neq$ *dynamical cache*). In addition, possessives tend to alternate with *of-PP form* (e.g. *agent's goal = goal of agent, security's value = value of security*).

4 Candidate Selection

We now describe our proposed candidate selection process. Candidate selection is a crucial step for automatic keyphrase extraction. This step is correlated to term extraction study since top N_{th} ranked terms become keyphrases in documents. In previous study, `KEA` employed the indexing words as candidates whereas others such as (Park et al., 2004; Nguyen and Kan, 2007) generated handcrafted regular expression rules. However, none carefully undertook the analysis of keyphrases. In this section, before we present our method, we first describe the detail of keyphrase analysis.

In our keyphrase analysis, we observed that most of *author assigned keyphrase* and/or *reader assigned keyphrase* are syntactically more often simplex words and less often NPs. When keyphrases take an NP form, they tend to be a simple form of NPs. i.e. either without a PP or with only a PP or with a conjunction, but few appear as a mixture of such forms. We also noticed that the components of NPs are normally nouns and adjectives but rarely, are adverbs and verbs. As a result, we decided to ignore NPs containing adverbs and verbs in this study as our candidates since they tend to produce more errors and to require more complexity.

Another observation is that keyphrases containing more than three words are rare (i.e. 6% in our data set), validating what Paukkeri et al. (2008) observed. Hence, we apply a *length heuristic*. Our candidate selection rule collects candidates up to length 3, but also of length 4 for NPs in *of-PP form*, since they may have a non-genetive alternation that reduces its length to 3 (e.g. *performance of distributed system = distributed system performance*). In previous studies, words occurring at least twice are selected as candidates. However, during our acquisition of *reader assigned keyphrase*, we observed that readers tend to collect NPs as keyphrases, regardless of their frequency. Due to this, we apply different frequency thresholds for simplex words ($>= 2$) and NPs ($>= 1$). Note that 30% of NPs occurred only once in our data.

Finally, we generated regular expression rules to extract candidates, as presented in Table 1. Our candidate extraction rules are based on those in Nguyen and Kan (2007). However, our **Rule6** for NPs in *of-PP form* broadens the coverage of possible candidates. i.e. with a given NPs in *of-PP form*, not only we collect simplex word(s), but we also extract non-*of-PP form* of NPs from noun phrases governing the PP and the PP. For example, our rule extracts *effective algorithm of grid computing* as well as *effective algorithm* and *grid computing* as candidates while the previous works' rules do not.

5 Feature Engineering

With a wider candidate selection criteria, the onus of filtering out irrelevant candidates becomes the responsibility of careful feature engineering. We list 25 features that we have found useful in extracting keyphrases, comprising of 9 existing and 16 novel and/or modified features that we introduce in our work (marked with $*$). As one of our goals in feature engineering is to assess the suitability of features in the unsupervised setting, we have also indicated which features are suitable only for the supervised setting (**S**) or applicable to both (**S, U**).

5.1 Document Cohesion

Document cohesion indicates how important the candidates are for the given document. The most popular feature for this cohesion is *TF*IDF* but some works have also used context words to check the correlation between candidates and the given document. Other features for document cohesion are *distance, section information* and so on. We note that listed features other than *TF*IDF* are related to locality. That is, the intuition behind these features is that keyphrases tend to appear in specific area such as the beginning and the end of documents.

F1 : TF*IDF *(S,U)* *TF*IDF* indicates document cohesion by looking at the frequency of terms in the documents and is broadly used in previous work(Frank et al., 1999; Witten et al., 1999; Nguyen and Kan, 2007). However, a disadvantage of the feature is in requiring a large corpus to compute useful *IDF*. As an alternative, context words(Matsuo and Ishizuka, 2004) can also be used to measure document cohesion. From our study of keyphrases, we saw that substrings within longer candidates need to be properly counted, and as such our method measures *TF* in substrings as well as in exact matches. For example, *grid computing* is often a substring of other phrases such as *grid computing algorithm* and *efficient grid computing algorithm*. We also normalize *TF* with respect to candidate types: i.e. we separately treat simplex words and NPs to compute *TF*. To make our *IDFs* broadly representative, we employed the `Google n-gram` counts, that were computed over terabytes of data. Given this large, generic source of word count, *IDF* can be incorporated without corpus-dependent processing, hence such features are useful in unsupervised approaches as well. The following list shows variations of *TF*IDF*, employed as features in our system.

- (F1a) *TF*IDF*
- (F1b*) *TF* including counts of substrings
- (F1c*) *TF* of substring as a separate feature
- (F1d*) normalized *TF* by candidate types (i.e. simplex words vs. NPs)
- (F1e*) normalized *TF* by candidate types as a separate feature
- (F1f*) *IDF* using `Google n-gram`

F2 : First Occurrence *(S,U)* `KEA` used the first appearance of the word in the document(Frank et al., 1999; Witten et al., 1999). The main idea behind this feature is that keyphrases tend to occur in the beginning of documents, especially in structured reports (e.g., in abstract and introduction sections) and newswire.

F3 : Section Information *(S,U)* Nguyen and Kan (2007) used the identity of which specific document section a candidate occurs in. This locality feature attempts to identify key sections. For example, in their study of scientific papers, the authors weighted candidates differently depending on whether they occurred in the abstract, introduction, conclusion, section head, title and/or references.

F4* : Additional Section Information *(S,U)* We first added the *related work or previous work* as one of section information not included in Nguyen and Kan (2007). We also propose and test a number of variations. We used the substrings that occur in section headers and reference titles as keyphrases. We counted the co-occurrence of candidates (i.e. the section *TF*) across all key sections that indicates the correlation among key sections. We assign section-specific weights as individual sections exhibit different propensities for generating keyphrases. For example, *introduction* contains the majority of keyphrases while the title or section head contains many fewer due to the variation in size.

- (F4a*) section, 'related/previous work'
- (F4b*) counting substring occurring in key sections
- (F4c*) section *TF* across all key sections
- (F4d*) weighting key sections according to the portion of keyphrases found

F5* : Last Occurrence *(S,U)* Similar to *distance* in KEA , the position of the last occurrence of a candidate may also imply the importance of keyphrases, as keyphrases tend to appear in the last part of document such as the conclusion and discussion.

5.2 Keyphrase Cohesion

The intuition behind using keyphrase cohesion is that actual keyphrases are often associated with each other, since they are semantically related to topic of the document. Note that this assumption holds only when the document describes a single, coherent topic – a document that represents a collection may be first need to be segmented into its constituent topics.

F6* : Co-occurrence of Another Candidate in Section *(S,U)* When candidates co-occur in several key sections together, then they are more likely keyphrases. Hence, we used the number of sections that candidates co-occur.

F7* : Title overlap *(S)* In a way, titles also represent the topics of their documents. A large collection of titles in the domain can act as a probabilistic prior of what words could stand as constituent words in keyphrases. In our work, as we examined scientific papers from computer science, we used a collection of titles obtained from the large *CiteSeer*[1] collection to create this feature.

- (F7a*) co-occurrence (Boolean) in title collocation
- (F7b*) co-occurrence (*TF*) in title collection

F8 : Keyphrase Cohesion *(S,U)* Turney (2003) integrated keyphrase cohesion into his system by checking the semantic similarity between top *N* ranked candidates against the remainder. In the original work, a large, external web corpus was used to obtain the similarity judgments. As we did not have access to the same web corpus and all candidates/keyphrases were not found in the Google n-gram corpus, we approximated this feature using a similar notion of contextual similarity. We simulated a latent 2-dimensional matrix (similar to latent semantic analysis) by listing all candidate words in rows and their neighboring words (nouns, verbs, and adjectives only) in columns. The cosine measure is then used to compute the similarity among keyphrases.

5.3 Term Cohesion

Term cohesion further refines the candidacy judgment, by incorporating an internal analysis of the candidate's constituent words. Term cohesion posits that high values for internal word association measures correlates indicates that the candidate is a keyphrase (Church and Hanks, 1989).

F9 : Term Cohesion *(S,U)* Park et al. (2004) used in the Dice coefficient (Dice, 1945) to measure term cohesion particularly for multiword terms. In their work, as NPs are longer than simplex words, they simply discounted simplex word cohesion by 10%. In our work, we vary the measure of *TF* used in Dice coefficient, similar to our discussion earlier.

- (F9a) term cohesion by (Park et al., 2004),
- (F9b*) normalized *TF* by candidate types (i.e. simplex words vs. NPs),
- (F9c*) applying different weight by candidate types,
- (F9d*) normalized *TF* and different weighting by candidate types

5.4 Other Features

F10 : Acronym *(S)* Nguyen and Kan (2007) accounted for the importance of *acronym* as a feature. We found that this feature is heavily dependent on the data set. Hence, we used it only for N&K to attest our *candidate selection method*.

F11 : POS sequence *(S)* Hulth and Megyesi (2006) pointed out that POS sequences of keyphrases are similar. It showed the distinctive distribution of POS sequences of keyphrases and use them as a feature. Like *acronym*, this is also subject to the data set.

[1]It contains 1.3M titles from articles, papers and reports.

F12 : Suffix sequence *(S)* Similar to *acronym*, Nguyen and Kan (2007) also used a candidate's *suffix sequence* as a feature, to capture the propensity of English to use certain Latin derivational morphology for technical keyphrases. This feature is also a data dependent features, thus used in supervised approach only.

F13 : Length of Keyphrases *(S, U)* Barker and Corrnacchia (2000) showed that candidate length is also a useful feature in extraction as well as in candidate selection, as the majority of keyphrases are one or two terms in length.

6 System and Data

To assess the performance of the proposed candidate selection rules and features, we implemented a keyphrase extraction pipe line. We start with raw text of computer science articles converted from *PDF* by `pdftotext`. Then, we partitioned the into section such as title and sections via heuristic rules and applied sentence segmenter [2], `ParsCit`[3](Councill et al., 2008) for reference collection, part-of-speech tagger[4] and lemmatizer[5](Minnen et al., 2001) of the input. After preprocessing, we built both supervised and unsupervised classifiers using Naive Bayes from the WEKA machine learning toolkit(Witten and Frank, 2005), Maximum Entropy[6], and simple weighting.

In evaluation, we collected 250 papers from four different categories[7] of the ACM digital library. Each paper was 6 to 8 pages on average. In *author assigned keyphrase*, we found many were missing or found as substrings. To remedy this, we collected *reader assigned keyphrase* by hiring senior year undergraduates in computer science, each whom annotated five of the papers with an annotation guideline and on average, took about 15 minutes to annotate each paper. The final statistics of keyphrases is presented in Table 2 where *Combined* represents the total number of keyphrases. The numbers in () denotes the number of keyphrases in *of-PP form*. *Found* means the number of *author assigned keyphrase* and *reader assigned keyphrase* found in the documents.

	Author	Reader	Combined
Total	1252 (53)	3110 (111)	3816 (146)
NPs	904	2537	3027
Average	3.85 (4.01)	12.44 (12.88)	15.26 (15.85)
Found	769	2509	2864

Table 2: Statistics in Keyphrases

7 Evaluation

The baseline system for both the supervised and unsupervised approaches is modified `N&K` which uses *TF*IDF*, *distance*, *section information* and *additional section information* (i.e. *F1-4*). Apart from `baseline` , we also implemented basic `KEA` and `N&K` to compare. Note that `N&K` is considered a supervised approach, as it utilizes features like *acronym, POS sequence*, and *suffix sequence*.

Table 3 and 4 shows the performance of our candidate selection method and features with respect to supervised and unsupervised approaches using the current standard evaluation method (i.e. exact matching scheme) over top $5_{th}, 10_{th}, 15_{th}$ candidates.

BestFeatures includes *F1c:TF of substring as a separate feature, F2:first occurrence, F3:section information, F4d:weighting key sections, F5:last occurrence, F6:co-occurrence of another candidate in section, F7b:title overlap, F9a:term cohesion by (Park et al., 2004), F13:length of keyphrases.* Best-TF*IDF means using all best features but *TF*IDF*.

In Tables 3 and 4, *C* denotes the classifier technique: unsupervised (*U*) or supervised using Maximum Entropy (*S*)[8].

In Table 5, the performance of each feature is measured using `N&K` system and the target feature. + indicates an improvement, - indicates a performance decline, and *?* indicates no effect or unconfirmed due to small changes of performances. Again, *supervised* denotes `Maximum Entropy` training and *Unsupervised* is our unsupervised approach.

8 Discussion

We compared the performances over our candidate selection and feature engineering with simple `KEA` , `N&K` and our baseline system. In evaluating candidate selection, we found that longer

[2]http://www.eng.ritsumei.ac.jp/asao/resources/sentseg/

[3]http://wing.comp.nus.edu.sg/parsCit/

[4]http://search.cpan.org/dist/Lingua-EN-Tagger/Tagger.pm

[5]http://www.informatics.susx.ac.uk/research/groups/nlp/carroll/morph.html

[6]http://maxent.sourceforge.net/index.html

[7]C2.4 (Distributed Systems), H3.3 (Information Search and Retrieval), I2.11 (Distributed Artificial Intelligence-Multiagent Systems) and J4 (Social and Behavioral Sciences-Economics)

[8]Due to the page limits, we present the best performance.

Method	Features	C	Five				Ten				Fifteen			
			Match	Precision	Recall	Fscore	Match	Precising	Recall	Fscore	Match	Precision	Recall	Fscore
All Candidates	KEA	U	0.03	0.64%	0.21%	0.32%	0.09	0.92%	0.60%	0.73%	0.13	0.88%	0.86%	0.87%
		S	0.79	15.84%	5.19%	7.82%	1.39	13.88%	9.09%	10.99%	1.84	12.24%	12.03%	12.13%
	N&K	S	1.32	26.48%	8.67%	13.06%	2.04	20.36%	13.34%	16.12%	2.54	16.93%	16.64%	16.78%
	baseline	U	0.92	18.32%	6.00%	9.04%	1.57	15.68%	10.27%	12.41%	2.20	14.64%	14.39%	14.51%
		S	1.15	23.04%	7.55%	11.37%	1.90	18.96%	12.42%	15.01%	2.44	16.24%	15.96%	16.10%
Length<=3 Candidates	KEA	U	0.03	0.64%	0.21%	0.32%	0.09	0.92%	0.60%	0.73%	0.13	0.88%	0.86%	0.87%
		S	0.81	16.16%	5.29%	7.97%	1.40	14.00%	9.17%	11.08%	1.84	12.24%	12.03%	12.13%
	N&K	S	1.40	27.92%	9.15%	13.78%	2.10	21.04%	13.78%	16.65%	2.62	17.49%	17.19%	17.34%
	baseline	U	0.92	18.4%	6.03%	9.08%	1.58	15.76%	10.32%	12.47%	2.20	14.64%	14.39%	14.51%
		S	1.18	23.68%	7.76%	11.69%	1.90	19.00%	12.45%	15.04%	2.40	16.00%	15.72%	15.86%
Length<=3 Candidates + Alternation	KEA	U	0.01	0.24%	0.08%	0.12%	0.05	0.52%	0.34%	0.41%	0.07	0.48%	0.47%	0.47%
		S	0.83	16.64%	5.45%	8.21%	1.42	14.24%	9.33%	11.27%	1.87	12.45%	12.24%	12.34%
	N&K	S	1.53	30.64%	10.04%	15.12%	2.31	23.08%	15.12%	18.27%	2.88	19.20%	18.87%	19.03%
	baseline	U	0.98	19.68%	6.45%	9.72%	1.72	17.24%	11.29%	13.64%	2.37	15.79%	15.51%	15.65%
		S	1.33	26.56%	8.70%	13.11%	2.09	20.88%	13.68%	16.53%	2.69	17.92%	17.61%	17.76%

Table 3: Performance on Proposed Candidate Selection

Features	C	Five				Ten				Fifteen			
		Match	Prec.	Recall	Fscore	Match	Prec.	Recall	Fscore	Match	Prec.	Recall	Fscore
Best	U	1.14	.228	.747	.113	1.92	.192	.126	.152	**2.61**	.174	.171	.173
	S	1.56	.312	.102	.154	2.50	.250	.164	.198	**3.15**	.210	.206	.208
Best w/o TF*IDF	U	1.14	.228	.74	.113	1.92	.192	.126	.152	**2.61**	.174	.171	.173
	S	1.56	.311	.102	.154	2.46	.246	.161	.194	**3.12**	.208	.204	.206

Table 4: Performance on Feature Engineering

A	Method	Feature
+	S	F1a,F2,F3,F4a,F4d,F9a
	U	F1a,F1c,F2,F3,F4a,F4d,F5,F7b,F9a
-	S	F1b,F1c,F1d,F1f,F4b,F4c,F7a,F7b,F9b-d,F13
	U	F1d,F1e,F1f,F4b,F4c,F6,F7a,F9b-d
?	S	F1e,F10,F11,F12
	U	F1b

Table 5: Performance on Each Feature

length candidates play a role to be noises so decreased the overall performance. We also confirmed that candidate alternation offered the flexibility of keyphrases leading higher candidate coverage as well as better performance.

To re-examine features, we analyzed the impact of existing and new features and their variations. First of all, unlike previous studies, we found that the performance with and without *TF*IDF* did not lead to a large difference which indicates the impact of *TF*IDF* was minor, as long as other features are incorporated. Secondly, counting substrings for *TF* improved performance, while applying term weighting for *TF* and/or *IDF* did not impact on the performance. We estimated the cause that many of keyphrases are substrings of candidates and vice versa. Thirdly, *section information* was also validated to improve performance, as in Nguyen and Kan (2007). Extending this logic, modeling additional section information (*related work*) and *weighting sections* both turned out to be useful features. Other locality features were also validated as helpful: both *first occurrence* and *last occurrence* are helpful as it implies the locality of the key ideas. In addition, keyphrase co-occurrence with selected sections was proposed in our work and found empirically useful. Term cohesion (Park et al., 2004) is a useful feature although it has a heuristic factor that reduce the weight by 10% for simplex words. Normally, term cohesion is subject to NPs only, hence it needs to be extended to work with multi-word NPs as well. Table 5 summarizes the reflections on each feature.

As unsupervised methods have the appeal of not needing to be trained on expensive hand-annotated data, we also compared the performance of supervised and unsupervised methods. Given the features initially introduced for supervised learning, unsupervised performance is surprisingly high. While supervised classifier produced a matching count of 3.15, the unsupervised classifier obtains a count of 2.61. We feel this indicates that the existing features for supervised methods are also suitable for use in unsupervised methods, with slightly reduced performance. In general, we observed that the best features in both supervised and unsupervised methods are the same – *section information* and *candidate length*. In our analysis of the impact of individual features, we observed that most features affect performance in the same way for both supervised and unsupervised approaches, as shown in Table 5. These findings indicate that although these features may be been originally designed for use in a supervised approach, they are stable and can be expected to perform similar in unsupervised approaches.

9 Conclusion

We have identified and tackled two core issues in automatic keyphrase extraction: candidate selection and feature engineering. In the area of candidate selection, we observe variations and alternations that were previously unaccounted for. Our selection rules expand the scope of possible keyphrase coverage, while not overly expanding the total number candidates to consider. In our re-examination of feature engineering, we compiled a comprehensive feature list from previous works while exploring the use of substrings in devising new features. Moreover, we also attested to each feature's fitness for use in unsupervised approaches, in order to utilize them in real-world applications with minimal cost.

10 Acknowledgement

This work was partially supported by a National Research Foundation grant, *Interactive Media Search* (grant # R 252 000 325 279), while the first author was a postdoctoral fellow at the National University of Singapore.

References

Ken Barker and Nadia Corrnacchia. Using noun phrase heads to extract document keyphrases. In *Proceedings of the 13th Biennial Conference of the Canadian Society on Computational Studies of Intelligence: Advances in Artificial Intelligence*. 2000.

Regina Barzilay and Michael Elhadad. Using lexical chains for text summarization. In *Proceedings of the ACL/EACL 1997 Workshop on Intelligent Scalable Text Summarization*. 1997, pp. 10–17.

Kenneth Church and Patrick Hanks. Word association norms, mutual information and lexicography. In Proceedings of ACL. 1989, 76–83.

Isaac Councill and C. Lee Giles and Min-Yen Kan. ParsCit: An open-source CRF reference string parsing package. In Proceedings of LREC. 2008, 28–30.

Ernesto DÁvanzo and Bernado Magnini. A Keyphrase-Based Approach to Summarization:the LAKE System at DUC-2005. In *Proceedings of DUC*. 2005.

F. Damerau. Generating and evaluating domain-oriented multi-word terms from texts. *Information Processing and Management*. 1993, 29, pp.43–447.

Lee Dice. Measures of the amount of ecologic associations between species. *Journal of Ecology*. 1945, 2.

Eibe Frank and Gordon Paynter and Ian Witten and Carl Gutwin and Craig Nevill-manning. Domain Specific Keyphrase Extraction. In *Proceedings of IJCAI*. 1999, pp.668–673.

Carl Gutwin and Gordon Paynter and Ian Witten and Craig Nevill-Manning and Eibe Frank. Improving browsing in digital libraries with keyphrase indexes. *Journal of Decision Support Systems*. 1999, 27, pp.81–104.

Khaled Hammouda and Diego Matute and Mohamed Kamel. CorePhrase: keyphrase extraction for document clustering. In *Proceedings of MLDM*. 2005.

Annette Hulth and Jussi Karlgren and Anna Jonsson and Henrik Bostrm and Lars Asker. Automatic Keyword Extraction using Domain Knowledge. In *Proceedings of CICLing*. 2001.

Annette Hulth and Beata Megyesi. A study on automatically extracted keywords in text categorization. In Proceedings of ACL/COLING. 2006, 537–544.

Mario Jarmasz and Caroline Barriere. Using semantic similarity over tera-byte corpus, compute the performance of keyphrase extraction. In *Proceedings of CLINE*. 2004.

Dawn Lawrie and W. Bruce Croft and Arnold Rosenberg. Finding Topic Words for Hierarchical Summarization. In *Proceedings of SIGIR*. 2001, pp. 349–357.

Y. Matsuo and M. Ishizuka. Keyword Extraction from a Single Document using Word Co-occurrence Statistical Information. In *International Journal on Artificial Intelligence Tools*. 2004, 13(1), pp. 157–169.

Olena Medelyan and Ian Witten. Thesaurus based automatic keyphrase indexing. In *Proceedings of ACM/IEED-CS joint conference on Digital libraries*. 2006, pp.296–297.

Guido Minnen and John Carroll and Darren Pearce. Applied morphological processing of English. *NLE*. 2001, 7(3), pp.207–223.

Thuy Dung Nguyen and Min-Yen Kan. Key phrase Extraction in Scientific Publications. In *Proceeding of ICADL*. 2007, pp.317-326.

Youngja Park and Roy Byrd and Branimir Boguraev. Automatic Glossary Extraction Beyond Terminology Identification. In *Proceedings of COLING*. 2004, pp.48–55.

Mari-Sanna Paukkeri and Ilari Nieminen and Matti Polla and Timo Honkela. A Language-Independent Approach to Keyphrase Extraction and Evaluation. In Proceedings of COLING. 2008.

Peter Turney. Learning to Extract Keyphrases from Text. In *National Research Council, Institute for Information Technology, Technical Report ERB-1057*. 1999.

Peter Turney. Coherent keyphrase extraction via Web mining. In *Proceedings of IJCAI*. 2003, pp. 434–439.

Xiaojun Wan and Jianguo Xiao. CollabRank: towards a collaborative approach to single-document keyphrase extraction. In *Proceedings of COLING*. 2008.

Ian Witten and Gordon Paynter and Eibe Frank and Car Gutwin and Graig Nevill-Manning. KEA:Practical Automatic Key phrase Extraction. In *Proceedings of ACM DL*. 1999, pp.254–256.

Ian Witten and Eibe Frank. Data Mining: Practical Machine Learning Tools and Techniques. Morgan Kaufmann, 2005.

Yongzheng Zhang and Nur Zinchir-Heywood and Evangelos Milios. Term based Clustering and Summarization of Web Page Collections. In *Proceedings of Conference of the Canadian Society for Computational Studies of Intelligence*. 2004.

Verb Noun Construction MWE Token Supervised Classification

Mona T. Diab
Center for Computational Learning Systems
Columbia University
mdiab@ccls.columbia.edu

Pravin Bhutada
Computer Science Department
Columbia University
pb2351@columbia.edu

Abstract

We address the problem of classifying multi-word expression tokens in running text. We focus our study on Verb-Noun Constructions (VNC) that vary in their idiomaticity depending on context. VNC tokens are classified as either idiomatic or literal. We present a supervised learning approach to the problem. We experiment with different features. Our approach yields the best results to date on MWE classification combining different linguistically motivated features, the overall performance yields an F-measure of 84.58% corresponding to an F-measure of 89.96% for idiomaticity identification and classification and 62.03% for literal identification and classification.

1 Introduction

In the literature in general a multiword expression (MWE) refers to a multiword unit or a collocation of words that co-occur together statistically more than chance. A MWE is a cover term for different types of collocations which vary in their transparency and fixedness. MWEs are pervasive in natural language, especially in web based texts and speech genres. Identifying MWEs and understanding their meaning is essential to language understanding, hence they are of crucial importance for any Natural Language Processing (NLP) applications that aim at handling robust language meaning and use. In fact, the seminal paper (Sag et al., 2002) refers to this problem as a *key* issue for the development of high-quality NLP applications.

For our purposes, a MWE is defined as a collocation of words that refers to a single concept, for example - *kick the bucket*, *spill the beans*, *make a decision*, etc. An MWE typically has an idiosyncratic meaning that is *more* or *different* from the meaning of its component words. An MWE meaning is transparent, i.e. predictable, in as much as the component words in the expression relay the meaning portended by the speaker compositionally. Accordingly, MWEs vary in their degree of meaning compositionality; compositionality is correlated with the level of idiomaticity. An MWE is compositional if the meaning of an MWE as a unit can be predicted from the meaning of its component words such as in *make a decision* meaning *to decide*. If we conceive of idiomaticity as being a continuum, the more idiomatic an expression, the less transparent and the more non-compositional it is. Some MWEs are more predictable than others, for instance, *kick the bucket*, when used idiomatically to mean *to die*, has nothing in common with the literal meaning of either *kick* or *bucket*, however, *make a decision* is very clearly related to *to decide*. Both of these expressions are considered MWEs but have varying degrees of compositionality and predictability. Both of these expressions belong to a class of idiomatic MWEs known as verb noun constructions (VNC). The first VNC *kick the bucket* is a non-decomposable VNC MWE, the latter *make a decision* is a decomposable VNC MWE. These types of constructions are the object of our study.

To date, most research has addressed the problem of MWE *type* classification for VNC expressions in English (Melamed, 1997; Lin, 1999; Baldwin et al., 2003; na Villada Moirón and Tiedemann, 2006; Fazly and Stevenson, 2007; Van de Cruys and Villada Moirón, 2007; McCarthy et al., 2007), not *token* classification. For example: *he spilt the beans on the kitchen counter* is most likely a literal usage. This is given away by the use of the prepositional phrase *on the kitchen counter*, as it is plausable that beans could have literally been spilt on a location such as a kitchen counter. Most previous research would classify *spilt the beans* as idiomatic irrespective of contextual usage. In a recent study by (Cook et al., 2008) of 53 idiom MWE types used in different contexts, the authors concluded that almost half of them had clear literal meaning and over 40% of their usages in text were actually literal. Thus, it would be important for an NLP application such as machine translation, for example, when given a new VNC MWE token, to be able to determine whether it is used idiomatically or not as it could potentially have detrimental effects on the quality of the translation.

Proceedings of the 2009 Workshop on Multiword Expressions, ACL-IJCNLP 2009, pages 17–22,
Suntec, Singapore, 6 August 2009. ©2009 ACL and AFNLP

In this paper, we address the problem of MWE classification for verb-noun (VNC) token constructions in running text. We investigate the binary classification of an unseen VNC token expression as being either **Idiomatic** (IDM) or **Literal** (LIT). An IDM expression is certainly an MWE, however, the converse is not necessarily true. To date most approaches to the problem of idiomaticity classification on the token level have been unsupervised (Birke and Sarkar, 2006; Diab and Krishna, 2009b; Diab and Krishna, 2009a; Sporleder and Li, 2009). In this study we carry out a supervised learning investigation using support vector machines that uses some of the features which have been shown to help in unsupervised approaches to the problem.

This paper is organized as follows: In Section 2 we describe our understanding of the various classes of MWEs in general. Section 3 is a summary of previous related research. Section 4 describes our approach. In Section 5 we present the details of our experiments. We discuss the results in Section 6. Finally, we conclude in Section 7.

2 Multi-word Expressions

MWEs are typically not productive, though they allow for inflectional variation (Sag et al., 2002). They have been conventionalized due to persistent use. MWEs can be classified based on their semantic types as follows. **Idiomatic**: This category includes expressions that are semantically non-compositional, *fixed expressions* such as *kingdom come, ad hoc, non-fixed expressions* such as *break new ground, speak of the devil*. The VNCs which we are focusing on in this paper fall into this category. **Semi-idiomatic**: This class includes expressions that seem semantically non-compositional, yet their semantics are more or less transparent. This category consists of Light Verb Constructions (LVC) such as *make a living* and Verb Particle Constructions (VPC) such as *write-up, call-up*. **Non-Idiomatic**: This category includes expressions that are semantically compositional such as *prime minister*, proper nouns such as *New York Yankees* and collocations such as *machine translation*. These expressions are *statistically idiosyncratic*. For instance, *traffic light* is the most likely lexicalization of the concept and would occur more often in text than, say, *traffic regulator* or *vehicle light*.

3 Related Work

Several researchers have addressed the problem of MWE classification (Baldwin et al., 2003; Katz and Giesbrecht, 2006; Schone and Juraksfy, 2001; Hashimoto et al., 2006; Hashimoto and Kawahara, 2008). The majority of the proposed research has been using unsupervised approaches and have addressed the problem of MWE type classification irrespective of usage in context (Fazly and Stevenson, 2007; Cook et al., 2007). We are aware of two supervised approaches to the problem: work by (Katz and Giesbrecht, 2006) and work by (Hashimoto and Kawahara, 2008).

In Katz and Giesbrecht (2006) (KG06) the authors carried out a vector similarity comparison between the context of an MWE and that of the constituent words using LSA to determine if the expression is idiomatic or not. The KG06 is similar in intuition to work proposed by (Fazly and Stevenson, 2007), however the latter work was unsupervised. KG06 experimented with a tiny data set of only 108 sentences corresponding to one MWE idiomatic expression.

Hashimoto and Kawahara (2008) (HK08) is the first large scale study to our knowledge that addressed token classification into idiomatic versus literal for Japanese MWEs of all types. They apply a supervised learning framework using support vector machines based on TinySVM with a quadratic kernel. They annotate a web based corpus for training data. They identify 101 idiom types each with a corresponding 1000 examples, hence they had a corpus of 102K sentences of annotated data for their experiments. They experiment with 90 idiom types only for which they had more than 50 examples. They use two types of features: word sense disambiguation (WSD) features and idiom features. The WSD features comprised some basic syntactic features such as POS, lemma information, token n-gram features, in addition to hypernymy information on words as well as domain information. For the idiom features they were mostly inflectional features such as voice, negativity, modality, in addition to adjacency and adnominal features. They report results in terms of accuracy and rate of error reduction. Their overall accuracy is of 89.25% using all the features.

4 Our Approach

We apply a supervised learning framework to the problem of both identifying and classifying a MWE expression token in context. We specifically focus on VNC MWE expressions. We use the annotated data by (Cook et al., 2008). We adopt a chunking approach to the problem using an Inside Outside Beginning (IOB) tagging framework for performing the identification of MWE VNC tokens and classifying them as idiomatic or literal in context. For chunk tagging, we use the Yam-

Cha sequence labeling system.[1] YamCha is based on Support Vector Machines technology using degree 2 polynomial kernels.

We label each sentence with standard IOB tags. Since this is a binary classification task, we have 5 different tags: B-L (Beginning of a literal chunk), I-L (Inside of a literal chunk), B-I (Beginning an Idiomatic chunk), I-I (Inside an Idiomatic chunk), O (Outside a chunk). As an example a sentence such as John kicked the bucket last Friday will be annotated as follows: John O, kicked B-I, the I-I, bucket I-I, last O, Friday O. We experiment with some basic features and some more linguistically motivated ones.

We experiment with different window sizes for context ranging from $-/+1$ to $-/+5$ tokens before and after the token of interest. We also employ linguistic features such as character n-gram features, namely last 3 characters of a token, as a means of indirectly capturing the word inflectional and derivational morphology (NGRAM). Other features include: Part-of-Speech (POS) tags, lemma form (LEMMA) or the citation form of the word, and named entity (NE) information. The latter feature is shown to help in the unsupervised setting in recent work (Diab and Krishna, 2009b; Diab and Krishna, 2009a). In general all the linguistic features are represented as separate feature sets explicitly modeled in the input data. Hence, if we are modeling the POS tag feature for our running example the training data would be annotated as follows: {John *NN* O, kicked *VBD* B-I, the *Det* I-I, bucket *NN* I-I, last *ADV* O, Friday *NN* O }. Likewise adding the NGRAM feature would be represented as follows: {John *NN ohn* O, kicked *VBD ked* B-I, the *Det the* I-I, bucket *NN ket* I-I, last *ADV ast* O, Friday *NN day* O.} and so on.

With the NE feature, we followed the same representation as the other features as a separate column as expressed above, referred to as Named Entity Separate (NES). For named entity recognition (NER) we use the BBN Identifinder software which identifies 19 NE tags.[2] We have two settings for NES: one with the full 19 tags explicitly identified (NES-Full) and the other where we have a binary feature indicating whether a word is a NE or not (NES-Bin). Moreover, we added another experimental condition where we changed the words' representation in the input to their NE class, Named Entity InText (NEI). For example for the NEI condition, our running example is represented as follows: {PER *NN ohn* O, kicked *VBD ked* B-I, the *Det the* I-I, bucket *NN ket* I-I, last *ADV ast* O, DAY *NN day* O}, where *John* is replaced by the NE "PER" .

[1] http://www.tado-chasen.com/yamcha

[2] http://www.bbn.com/identifinder

5 Experiments and Results

5.1 Data

We use the manually annotated standard data set identified in (Cook et al., 2008). This data comprises 2920 unique VNC-Token expressions drawn from the entire British National Corpus (BNC).[3] The BNC contains 100M words of multiple genres including written text and transcribed speech. In this set, VNC token expressions are manually annotated as *idiomatic*, *literal* or *unknown*. We exclude those annotated as *unknown* and those pertaining to the Speech part of the data leaving us with a total of 2432 sentences corresponding to 53 VNC MWE types. This data has 2571 annotations,[4] corresponding to 2020 Idiomatic tokens and 551 literal ones. Since the data set is relatively small we carry out 5-fold cross validation experiments. The results we report are averaged over the 5 folds per condition. We split the data into 80% for training, 10% for testing and 10% for development. The data used is the tokenized version of the BNC.

5.2 Evaluation Metrics

We use $F_{\beta=1}$ (F-measure) as the harmonic mean between (P)recision and (R)ecall, as well as accuracy to report the results.[5] We report the results separately for the two classes IDM and LIT averaged over the 5 folds of the TEST data set.

5.3 Results

We present the results for the different features sets and their combination. We also present results on a simple most frequent tag baseline (FREQ) as well as a baseline of using no features, just the tokenized words (TOK). The baseline is basically tagging all *identified* VNC tokens in the data set as idiomatic. It is worth noting that the baseline has the advantage of gold identification of MWE VNC token expressions. In our experimental conditions, identification of a potential VNC MWE is part of what is discovered automatically, hence our system is penalized for identifying other VNC MWE

[3] http://www.natcorp.ox.ac.uk/

[4] A sentence can have more than one MWE expression hence the number of annotations exceeds the number of sentences.

[5] We do not think that accuracy should be reported in general since it is an inflated result as it is not a measure of error. All words identified as O factor into the accuracy which results in exaggerated values for accuracy. We report it only since it the metric used by previous work.

tokens that are not in the original data set.[6]

In Table 2 we present the results yielded per feature and per condition. We experimented with different context sizes initially to decide on the optimal window size for our learning framework, results are presented in Table 1. Then once that is determined, we proceed to add features.

Noting that a window size of $-/+3$ yields the best results, we proceed to use that as our context size for the following experimental conditions. We will not include accuracy since it above 96% for all our experimental conditions.

All the results yielded by our experiments outperform the baseline FREQ. The simple tokenized words baseline (TOK) with no added features with a context size of $-/+3$ shows a significant improvement over the very basic baseline FREQ with an overall F measure of 77.04%.

Adding lemma information or POS or NGRAM features all independently contribute to a better solution, however combining the three features yields a significant boost in performance over the TOK baseline of 2.67% absolute F points in overall performance.

Confirming previous observations in the literature, the overall best results are obtained by using NE features. The NEI condition yields slightly better results than the NES conditions in the case when no other features are being used. NES-Full significantly outperforms NES-Bin when used alone especially on literal classification yielding the highest results on this class of phenomena across the board. However when combined with other features, NES-Bin fares better than NES-Full as we observe slightly less performance when comparing NES-Full+L+N+P and NES-Bin+L+N+P.

Combining NEI+L+N+P yields the highest results with an overall F measure of 84.58% a significant improvement over both baselines and over the condition that does not exploit NE features, L+N+P. Using NEI may be considered a form of dimensionality reduction hence the significant contribution to performance.

6 Discussion

The overall results strongly suggest that using linguistically interesting features explicitly has a positive impact on performance. NE features help the most and combining them with other features yields the best results. In general performance on the classification and identification of idiomatic expressions yielded much better results. This may be due to the fact that the data has a lot more idiomatic token examples for training. Also we note that precision scores are significantly higher than recall scores especially with performance on literal token instance classification. This might be an indication that identifying when an MWE is used literally is a difficult task.

We analyzed some of the errors yielded in our best condition NEI+L+N+P. The biggest errors are a result of identifying other VNC constructions not annotated in the training and test data as VNC MWEs. However, we also see errors of confusing idiomatic cases with literal ones 23 times, and the opposite 4 times.

Some of the errors where the VNC should have been classified as literal however the system classified them as idiomatic are *k*ick heel, find feet, make top. Cases of idiomatic expressions erroneously classified as literal are for MWE types *h*it the road, blow trumpet, blow whistle, bit a wall.

The system is able to identify new VNC MWE constructions. For instance in the sentence *On the other hand Pinkie seemed to have* **lost his head** *to a certain extent perhaps some prospects of* **making his mark** *by bringing in something novel in the way of business*, the first MWE **lost his head** is annotated in the training data, however **making his mark** is newly identified as idiomatic in this context.

Also the system identified **hit the post** as a literal MWE VNC token in *As the ball* **hit the post** *the referee* **blew the whistle**, where **blew the whistle** is a literal VNC in this context and it identified **hit the post** as another literal VNC.

7 Conclusion

In this study, we explore a set of features that contribute to VNC token expression binary supervised classification. The use of NER significantly improves the performance of the system. Using NER as a means of dimensionality reduction yields the best results. We achieve a state of the art performance of an overall F measure of 84.58%. In the future we are looking at ways of adding more sophisticated syntactic and semantic features from WSD. Given the fact that we were able to get more interesting VNC data automatically, we are currently looking into adding the new data to the annotated pool after manual checking.

[6]We could have easily identified all VNC syntactic configurations corresponding to verb object as a potential MWE VNC assuming that they are literal by default. This would have boosted our literal score baseline, however, for this investigation, we decided to strictly work with the gold standard data set exclusively.

	IDM-F	LIT-F	Overall F	Overall Acc.
−/+1	77.93	48.57	71.78	96.22
−/+2	85.38	55.61	79.71	97.06
−/+3	**86.99**	**55.68**	**81.25**	96.93
−/+4	86.22	55.81	80.75	97.06
−/+5	83.38	50	77.63	96.61

Table 1: Results in %s of varying context window size

	IDM-P	IDM-R	IDM-F	LIT-P	LIT-R	LIT-F	Overall F
FREQ	70.02	89.16	78.44	0	0	0	69.68
TOK	81.78	83.33	82.55	71.79	43.75	54.37	77.04
(L)EMMA	83.1	84.29	83.69	69.77	46.88	56.07	78.11
(N)GRAM	83.17	82.38	82.78	70	43.75	53.85	77.01
(P)OS	83.33	83.33	83.33	77.78	43.75	56.00	78.08
L+N+P	86.95	83.33	85.38	72.22	45.61	55.91	79.71
NES-Full	85.2	87.93	86.55	79.07	**58.62**	**67.33**	82.77
NES-Bin	84.97	82.41	83.67	73.49	52.59	61.31	79.15
NEI	89.92	85.18	87.48	81.33	52.59	63.87	82.82
NES-Full+L+N+P	89.89	84.92	87.34	76.32	50	60.42	81.99
NES-Bin+L+N+P	90.86	84.92	87.79	76.32	50	60.42	82.33
NEI+L+N+P	**91.35**	**88.42**	**89.86**	**81.69**	50	62.03	**84.58**

Table 2: Final results in %s averaged over 5 folds of test data using different features and their combinations

8 Acknowledgement

The first author was partially funded by DARPA GALE and MADCAT projects. The authors would like to acknowledge the useful comments by two anonymous reviewers who helped in making this publication more concise and better presented.

References

Timothy Baldwin, Collin Bannard, Takakki Tanaka, and Dominic Widdows. 2003. An empirical model of multiword expression decomposability. In *Proceedings of the ACL 2003 workshop on Multiword expressions*, pages 89–96, Morristown, NJ, USA.

J. Birke and A. Sarkar. 2006. A clustering approach for nearly unsupervised recognition of nonliteral language. In *Proceedings of EACL*, volume 6, pages 329–336.

Paul Cook, Afsaneh Fazly, and Suzanne Stevenson. 2007. Pulling their weight: Exploiting syntactic forms for the automatic identification of idiomatic expressions in context. In *Proceedings of the Workshop on A Broader Perspective on Multiword Expressions*, pages 41–48, Prague, Czech Republic, June. Association for Computational Linguistics.

Paul Cook, Afsaneh Fazly, and Suzanne Stevenson. 2008. The VNC-Tokens Dataset. In *Proceedings of the LREC Workshop on Towards a Shared Task for Multiword Expressions (MWE 2008)*, Marrakech, Morocco, June.

Mona Diab and Madhav Krishna. 2009a. Handling sparsity for verb noun MWE token classification. In *Proceedings of the Workshop on Geometrical Models of Natural Language Semantics*, pages 96–103, Athens, Greece, March. Association for Computational Linguistics.

Mona Diab and Madhav Krishna. 2009b. Unsupervised classification for vnc multiword expressions tokens. In *CICLING*.

Afsaneh Fazly and Suzanne Stevenson. 2007. Distinguishing subtypes of multiword expressions using linguistically-motivated statistical measures. In *Proceedings of the Workshop on A Broader Perspective on Multiword Expressions*, pages 9–16, Prague, Czech Republic, June. Association for Computational Linguistics.

Chikara Hashimoto and Daisuke Kawahara. 2008. Construction of an idiom corpus and its application to idiom identification based on WSD incorporating idiom-specific features. In *Proceedings of the 2008 Conference on Empirical Methods in Natural Language Processing*, pages 992–1001, Honolulu, Hawaii, October. Association for Computational Linguistics.

Chikara Hashimoto, Satoshi Sato, and Takehito Utsuro. 2006. Japanese idiom recognition: Drawing a line between literal and idiomatic meanings. In *Proceedings of the COLING/ACL 2006 Main Conference*

Poster Sessions, pages 353–360, Sydney, Australia, July. Association for Computational Linguistics.

Graham Katz and Eugenie Giesbrecht. 2006. Automatic identification of non-compositional multiword expressions using latent semantic analysis. In *Proceedings of the Workshop on Multiword Expressions: Identifying and Exploiting Underlying Properties*, pages 12–19, Sydney, Australia, July. Association for Computational Linguistics.

Dekang Lin. 1999. Automatic identification of non-compositional phrases. In *Proceedings of ACL-99*, pages 317–324, Univeristy of Maryland, College Park, Maryland, USA.

Diana McCarthy, Sriram Venkatapathy, and Aravind Joshi. 2007. Detecting compositionality of verb-object combinations using selectional preferences. In *Proceedings of the 2007 Joint Conference on Empirical Methods in Natural Language Processing and Computational Natural Language Learning (EMNLP-CoNLL)*, pages 369–379, Prague, Czech Republic, June. Association for Computational Linguistics.

Dan I. Melamed. 1997. Automatic discovery of non-compositional compounds in parallel data. In *Proceedings of the 2nd Conference on Empirical Methods in Natural Language Processing (EMNLP'97)*, pages 97–108, Providence, RI, USA, August.

Bego na Villada Moirón and Jörg Tiedemann. 2006. Identifying idiomatic expressions using automatic word-alignment. In *Proceedings of the EACL-06 Workshop on Multiword Expressions in a Multilingual Context*, pages 33–40, Morristown, NJ, USA.

Ivan A. Sag, Timothy Baldwin, Francis Bond, Ann A. Copestake, and Dan Flickinger. 2002. Multiword expressions: A pain in the neck for nlp. In *Proceedings of the Third International Conference on Computational Linguistics and Intelligent Text Processing*, pages 1–15, London, UK. Springer-Verlag.

Patrick Schone and Daniel Juraksfy. 2001. Is knowledge-free induction of multiword unit dictionary headwords a solved problem? In *Proceedings of Empirical Methods in Natural Language Processing*, pages 100–108, Pittsburg, PA, USA.

C. Sporleder and L. Li. 2009. Unsupervised Recognition of Literal and Non-Literal Use of Idiomatic Expressions. In *Proceedings of the 12th Conference of the European Chapter of the ACL (EACL 2009)*, pages 754–762. Association for Computational Linguistics.

Tim Van de Cruys and Begoña Villada Moirón. 2007. Semantics-based multiword expression extraction. In *Proceedings of the Workshop on A Broader Perspective on Multiword Expressions*, pages 25–32, Prague, Czech Republic, June. Association for Computational Linguistics.

Exploiting Translational Correspondences for Pattern-Independent MWE Identification

Sina Zarrieß
Department of Linguistics
University of Potsdam, Germany
sina@ling.uni-potsdam.de

Jonas Kuhn
Department of Linguistics
University of Potsdam, Germany
kuhn@ling.uni-potsdam.de

Abstract

Based on a study of verb translations in the Europarl corpus, we argue that a wide range of MWE patterns can be identified in translations that exhibit a correspondence between a single lexical item in the source language and a group of lexical items in the target language. We show that these correspondences can be reliably detected on dependency-parsed, word-aligned sentences. We propose an extraction method that combines word alignment with syntactic filters and is independent of the structural pattern of the translation.

1 Introduction

Parallel corpora have proved to be a valuable resource not only for statistical machine translation, but also for crosslingual induction of morphological, syntactic and semantic analyses (Yarowsky et al., 2001; Dyvik, 2004). In this paper, we propose an approach to the identification of multiword expressions (MWEs) that exploits translational correspondences in a parallel corpus. We will consider in translations of the following type:

(1) Der Rat sollte unsere Position **berücksichtigen**.
The Council should our position consider.

(2) The Council should **take account of** our position.

This sentence pair has been taken from the German - English section of the Europarl corpus (Koehn, 2005). It exemplifies a translational correspondence between an English MWE *take account of* and a German simplex verb *berücksichtigen*. In the following, we refer to such correspondences as **one-to-many translations**. Based on a study of verb translations in Europarl, we will explore to what extent one-to-many translations provide evidence for MWE realization in the target language. It will turn out that crosslingual correspondences realize a wide range of different linguistic patterns that are relevant for MWE identification, but that they pose problems to automatic word alignment. We propose an extraction method that combines distributional word alignment with syntactic filters. We will show that these correspondences can be reliably detected on dependency-parsed, wordaligned sentences and are able to identify various MWE patterns.

In a monolingual setting, the task of MWE extraction is usually conceived of as a lexical association problem where distributional measures model the syntactic and semantic idiosyncracy exhibited by MWEs, e.g. (Pecina, 2008). This approach generally involves two main steps: 1) the extraction of a candidate list of potential MWEs, often constrained by a particular target pattern of the detection method, like verb particle constructions (Baldwin and Villavicencio, 2002) or verb PP combinations (Villada Moirón and Tiedemann, 2006), 2) the ranking of this candidate list by an appropriate assocation measure.

The crosslingual MWE identification we present in this paper is, a priori, independent of any specific association measure or syntactic pattern. The translation scenario allows us to adopt a completely data-driven definition of what constitutes an MWE: Given a parallel corpus, we propose to consider those tokens in a target language as MWEs which correspond to a single lexical item in the source language. The intuition is that if a group of lexical items in one language can be realized as a single item in another language, it can be considered as some kind of lexically fixed entity. By this means, we will not approach the MWE identification problem by asking for a given list of candidates whether these are MWEs or not. Instead, we will ask for a given list of lexical items in a source language whether there exists a one-to-many translation for this item in a target language (and whether these

Proceedings of the 2009 Workshop on Multiword Expressions, ACL-IJCNLP 2009, pages 23–30,
Suntec, Singapore, 6 August 2009.

one-to-many translations correspond to MWEs). This strategy offers a straightforward solution to the interpretation problem: As the translation can be related to the meaning of the source item and to its other translations in the target language, the interpretation is independent of the expression's transparency. This solution has its limitations compared to other approaches that need to automatically establish the degree of compositionality of a given MWE candidate. However, for many NLP applications, coarse-grained knowledge about the semantic relation between a wide range of MWEs and their corresponding atomic realization is already very useful.

In this work, we therefore focus on a general method of MWE identification that captures the various patterns of translational correspondences that can be found in parallel corpora. Our experiments described in section 3 show that one-to-many translations should be extracted from syntactic configurations rather than from unstructured sets of aligned words. This syntax-driven method is less dependent on frequency distributions in a given corpus, but is based on the intuition that monolingual idiosyncracies like MWE realization of an entity are not likely to be mirrored in another language (see section 4 for discussion).

Our goal in this paper is twofold: First, we want to investigate to what extent one-to-many translational correspondences can serve as an empirical basis for MWE identification. To this end, Section 2 presents a corpus-based study of the relation between one-to-many translations and MWEs that we carried out on a translation gold standard. Second, we investigate methods for the automatic detection of complex lexical correspondences for a given parallel corpus. Therefore, Section 3 evaluates automatic word alignments against our gold standard and gives a method for high-precision one-to-many translation detection that relies on syntactic filters, in addition to word-alignments.

2 Multiword Translations as MWEs

The idea to exploit one-to-many translations for the identification of MWE candidates has not received much attention in the literature. Thus, it is not a priori clear what can be expected from translational correspondences with respect to MWE identification. To corroborate the intuitions introduced in the last section, we carried out a corpus-based study that aims to discover linguistic patterns exhibited by one-to-many translations.

Verb	1-1	1-n	n-1	n-n	N_o
anheben (v_1)	53.5	21.2	9.2	16	325
bezwecken (v_2)	16.7	51.3	0.6	31.3	150
riskieren (v_3)	46.7	35.7	0.5	17	182
verschlimmern (v_4)	30.2	21.5	28.6	44.5	275

Table 1: Proportions of types of translational correspondences (token-level) in our gold standard.

We constructed a gold standard covering *all* English translations of four German verb lemmas extracted from the Europarl Corpus. These verbs subcategorize for a nominative subject and an accusative object and are in the middle frequency layer (around 200 occurrences). We extracted all sentences in Europarl with occurences of these lemmas and their automatic word alignments produced by GIZA++ (Och and Ney, 2003). These alignments were manually corrected on the basis of the crosslingual word alignment guidelines developped by (Graça et al., 2008).

For each of the German source lemmas, our gold standard records four translation categories: one-to-one, one-to-many, many-to-one, many-to-many translations. Table 1 shows the distribution of these categories for each verb. Strikingly, the four verbs show very different proportions concerning the types of their translational correspondences. Thus, while the German verb *anheben* (en. *increase*) seems to have a frequent parallel realization, the verbs *bezwecken* (en. *intend to*) or *verschlimmern* (en. *aggravate*) tend to be realized by more complex phrasal translations. In any case, the percentage of one-to-many translations is relatively high which corroborates our hypothesis that parallel corpora constitute a very interesting resource for data-driven MWE discovery.

A closer look at the one-to-many translations reveals that these cover a wide spectrum of MWE phenomena traditionally considered in the literature, as well as constructions that one would usually not regard as an MWE. Below, we will shortly illustrate the different classes of one-to-many translations we found in our gold standard.

Morphological variations: This type of one-to-many translations is mainly due to non-parallel realization of tense. It's rather irrelevant from an MWE perspective, but easy to discover and filter automatically.

(3) Sie **verschlimmern** die Übel.
They aggravate the misfortunes.

(4) Their action **is aggravating** the misfortunes.

Verb particle combinations: A typical MWE pattern, treated for instance in (Baldwin and Villavicencio, 2002). It further divides into transparent and non-transparent combinations, the latter is illustrated below.

(5) Der Ausschuss **bezweckt**, den Institutionen ein
The committe intends, the institutions a
politisches Instrument an die Hand zu geben.
political instrument at the hand to give.

(6) The committee **set out** to equip the institutions with a political instrument.

Verb preposition combinations: While this class isn't discussed very often in the MWE literature, it can nevertheless be considered as an idiosyncratic combination of lexical items. Sag et al (2002) propose an analysis within an MWE framework.

(7) Sie werden den Treibhauseffekt **verschlimmern**.
They will the green house effect aggravate.

(8) They will **add to** the green house effect.

Light verb constructions (LVCs): This is the most frequent pattern in our gold standard. It actually subsumes various subpatterns depending on whether the light verbs complement is realized as a noun, adjective or PP. Generally, LVCs are syntactically and semantically more flexible than other MWE types, such that our gold standard contains variants of LVCs with similar, potentially modified adjectives or nouns, as in the example below. However, it can be considered an idiosyncratic combination since the LVCs exhibit specific lexical restrictions (Sag et al., 2002).

(9) Ich werde die Sache nur noch **verschlimmern**.
Ich will the thing only just aggravate.

(10) I am just **making** things **more difficult**.

Idioms: This MWE type is probably the most discussed in the literature due to its semantic and syntactic idiosyncracy. It's not very frequent in our gold standard which may be mainly due to its limited size and the source items we chose.

(11) Sie **bezwecken** die Umgestaltung in eine zivile
They intend the conversion into a civil
Nation.
nation.

(12) They **have in mind** the conversion into a civil nation.

	v_1	v_2	v_3	v_4
N_{type}	22 (26)	41 (47)	26 (35)	17 (24)
V Part	22.7	4.9	0.0	0.0
V Prep	36.4	41.5	3.9	5.9
LVC	18.2	29.3	88.5	88.2
Idiom	0.0	2.4	0.0	0.0
Para	36.4	24.3	11.5	23.5

Table 2: Proportions of MWE types per lemma

Paraphrases: From an MWE perspective, paraphrases are the most problematic and challenging type of translational correspondence in our gold standard. While the MWE literature typically discusses the distinction between collocations and MWEs, the boarderline between paraphrases and MWEs is not really clear. On the hand, paraphrases, as we classified them here, are transparent combinations of lexical items, like in the example below *ensure that something increases*. However, semantically, these transparent combinations can also be rendered by an atomic expression *increase*. A further problem raised by paraphrases is that they often involve translational shifts (Cyrus, 2006). These shifts are hard to identify automatically and present a general challenge for semantic processing of parallel corpora. An example is given below.

(13) Wir brauchen bessere Zusammenarbeit, um die
We need better cooperation to the
Rückzahlungen **anzuheben** .
repayments.OBJ increase.

(14) We need greater cooperation in this respect to **ensure that** repayments **increase** .

Table 2 displays the proportions of the MWE categories for the number of types of one-to-many correspondences in our gold standard. We filtered the types due to morphological variations only (the overall number of types is indicated in brackets). Note that some types in our gold standard fall into several categories, e.g. they combine a verb preposition with a verb particle construction. For all of the verbs, the number of types belonging to core MWE categories largely outweighs the proportion of paraphrases. As we already observed in our analysis of general translation categories, here again, the different verb lemmas show striking differences with respect to their realization in English translations. For instance, *anheben* (en. *increase*) or *bezwecken* (en. *intend*) are frequently translated with verb particle or preposition combinations, while the other verbs are much more often translated by means of LVCs. Also, the more specific LVC patterns differ largely among the verbs. While *verschlimmern* (en. *aggravate*) has many different adjectival LVC correspondences, the translations of *riskieren* (en. *risk*) are predominantly nominal LVCs. The fact that we found very few idioms in our gold standard may be simply related to our arbitrary choice of German source verbs that do not have an English idiom realization (see our experiment on a random set of verbs in Section 3.3).

In general, one-to-many translational correspondences seem to provide a very fruitful ground for the large-scale study of MWE phenomena. However, their reliable detection in parallel corpora is far from trivial, as we will show in the next section. Therefore, we will not further investigate the classification of MWE patterns in the rest of the paper, but concentrate on the high-precision detection of one-to-many translations. Such a pattern-independent identification method is crucial for the further data-driven study of one-to-many translations in parallel corpora.

3 Multiword Translation Detection

This section is devoted to the problem of high-precision detection of one-to-many translations. Section 3.1 describes an evaluation of automatic word alignments against our gold standard. In section 3.2, we describe a method that extracts loosely aligned syntactic configurations which yields much more promising results.

3.1 One-to-many Alignments

To illustrate the problem of purely distributional one-to-many alignment, table 3 presents an evaluation of the automatic one-to-many word alignments produced by GIZA++ that uses the standard heuristics for bidirectional word alignment from phrase-based MT (Och and Ney, 2003). We evaluate the rate of translational correspondences on the type-level that the system discovers against the one-to-many translations in our gold standard. By *type* we mean the set of lemmatized English tokens that makes up the translation of the German source lemma. Generally, automatic word alignment yields a very high FPR if no frequency threshold is used. Increasing the threshold may help in some cases, however the frequency of the translation types is so low, that already at a threshold of 3, almost all types get filtered. This does not mean that the automatic word alignment does not discover any correct correspondences at all, but it means that the detection of the exact set of tokens that correspond to the source token is rare.

verb	n > 0		n > 1		n > 3	
	FPR	FNR	FPR	FNR	FPR	FNR
v_1	0.97	0.93	1.0	1.0	1.0	1.0
v_2	0.93	0.9	0.5	0.96	0.0	0.98
v_3	0.88	0.83	0.8	0.97	0.67	0.97
v_4	0.98	0.92	0.8	0.92	0.34	0.92

Table 3: False positive rate and False negative rate of GIZA++ one-to-many alignments

This low precision of one-to-many alignments isn't very surprising. Many types of MWEs consist of items that contribute most of the lexical semantic content, while the other items belong to the class of semantically almost "empty" items (e.g. particles, light verbs). These semantically "light" items have a distribution that doesn't necessarily correlate with the source item. For instance, in the following sentence pair taken from Europarl, GIZA++ was not able to capture the correspondence between the German main verb *behindern* (en. *impede*) and the LVC *constitute an obstacle to*, but only finds an alignment link between the verb and the noun *obstacle*.

(15) Die Korruption **behindert** die Entwicklung.
The corruption impedes the development.

(16) Corruption **constitutes an obstacle to** development.

Another limitation of the word-alignment models is that are independent of whether the sentences are largely parallel or rather free translations. However, parallel corpora like Europarl are know to contain a very large number of free translations. In these cases, direct lexical correspondences are much more unlikely to be found.

3.2 Aligning Syntactic Configurations

High-precision extraction of one-to-many translation detection thus involves two major problems: 1) How to identify sentences or configurations where reliable lexical correspondences can be found? 2) How to align target items that have a low occurrence correlation?

We argue that both of these problems can be adressed by taking syntactic information into account. As an example, consider the pair of parallel configurations in Figure 1 for the sentence pair given in (15) and (16). Although there is no strict one-to-one alignment for the German verb, the basic predicate-argument structure is parallel: The verbs arguments directly correspond to each other and are all dominated by a verbal root node.

Based on these intuitions, we propose a generate-and-filter strategy for our one-to-many translation detection which extracts partial, largely parallel dependency configurations. By admitting target dependency paths to be aligned to source single dependency relations, we admit configurations where the source item is translated by more than one word. For instance, given the configuration in Figure 1, we allow the German verb to be aligned to the path connecting *constitute* and the argument Y_2.

Our one-to-many translation detection consists of the following steps: a) candidate generation of aligned syntactic configurations, b) filtering the configurations c) alignment post-editing, i.e. assembling the target tokens corresponding to the source item. The following paragraphs will briefly caracterize these steps.

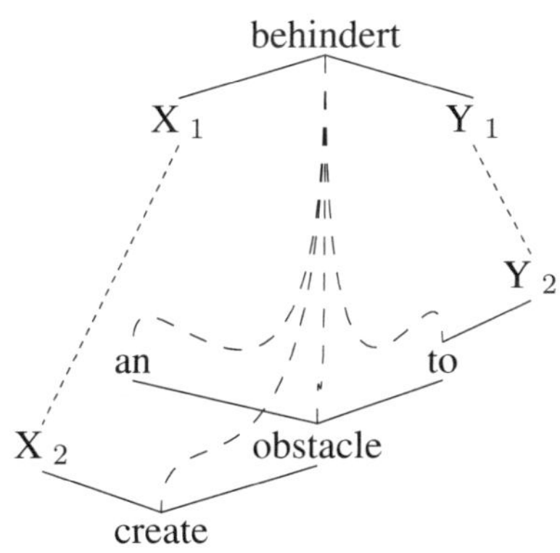

Figure 1: Example of a typical syntactic MWE configuration

Data We word-aligned the German and English portion of the Europarl corpus by means of the GIZA++ tool. Both portions where assigned flat syntactic dependency analyses by means of the MaltParser (Nivre et al., 2006) such that we obtain a parallel resource of word-aligned dependency parses. Each sentence in our resource can be represented by the triple $(D_G, D_E, A_{G,E})$. D_G is the set of dependency triples (s_1, rel, s_2) such that s_2 is a dependent of s_1 of type rel and s_1, s_2 are words of the source language. D_E is the set of dependency triples of the target sentence. $A_{G,E}$ corresponds to the set of pairs (s_1, t_1) such that s_1, t_1 are aligned.

Candidate Generation This step generates a list of source configurations by searching for occurences of the source lexical verb where it is linked to some syntactic dependents (e.g. its arguments). An example input would be the configuration `( (verb,SB,%), (verb,OA,%))` for our German verbs.

Filtering Given our source candidates, a valid parallel configuration $(D_G, D_E, A_{G,E})$ is then defined by the following conditions:

1. The source configuration D_G is the set of tuples (s_1, rel, s_n) where s_1 is our source item and s_n some dependent.
2. For each $s_n \in D_G$, there is a tuple $(s_n, t_n) \in A_{G,E}$, i.e. every dependent has an alignment.
3. There is a target item $t_1 \in D_E$ such that for each t_n, there is a $p \subset D_E$ such that p is a path $(t_1, rel, t_x), (t_x, rel, t_y) ... (t_z, rel, t_n)$ that connects t_1 and t_n. Thus, the target dependents have a common root.

To filter noise due to parsing or alignment errors, we further introduce a filter on the length of the path that connects the target root and its dependents and w exclude paths cross contain sentence boundaries. Moreover, the above candidate filtering doesn't exclude configurations which exhibit paraphrases involving head-switching or complex coordination. Head-switching can be detected with the help of alignment information: if there is a item in our target configuration that has an reliable alignment with an item not contained in our source configuration, our target configuration is likely to contain such a structural paraphrases and is excluded from our candidate set. Coordination can be discarded by imposing the condition on the configuration not to contain a coordination relation. This Generate-and-Filter strategy now extracts a set of sentences where we are likely to find a good one-to-one or one-to-many translation for the source verb.

Alignment Post-editing In the final alignment step, one now needs to figure out which lexical material in the aligned syntactic configurations actually corresponds to the translation of the source item. The intuition discussed in 3.2 was that all the items lying on a path between the root item and the terminals belong to the translation of the source item. However, these items may have other syntactic dependents that may also be part of the one-to-many translation. As an example, consider the configuration in figure 1 where the article *an* which is part of the LVC *create an obstacle to* has to be aligned to the German source verb.

Thus, for a set of items t_i for which there is a dependency relation $(t_x, rel, t_i) \in D_E$ such that t_x is an element of our target configuration, we need to decide whether $(s_1, t_i) \in A_{G,E}$. This translation problem now largely parallels collocation translation problems discussed in the literature, as in (Smadja and McKeown, 1994). But, crucially, our syntactic filtering strategy has substantially narrowed down the number of items that are possible parts of the one-to-many translation. Thus, a straightforward way to assemble the translational correspondence is to compute the correlation or association of the possibly missing items with the given translation pair as proposed in (Smadja and McKeown, 1994). Therefore, we propose the following alignment post-editing algorithm:
Given the source item s_1 and the set of target items T, where each $t_i \in T$ is an element of our target configuration,

1. Compute $corr(s_1, T)$, the correlation between s_1 and T.

2. For each t_i, t_x such that there is a $(t_i, rel, t_x) \in D_E$, compute $corr(s_1, T + \{t_x\})$

3. if $corr(s_1, T + \{t_x\}) \geq corr(s_1, T)$, add t_x to T.

As the Dice coefficient is often to give the best results, e.g. in (Smadja and McKeown, 1994), we also chose Dice as our correlation measure. In future work, we will experiment with other association measures. Our correlation scores are thus defined by the formula:

$$corr(s_1, T) = \frac{2(freq(s_1 \wedge T))}{freq(s_1) + freq(T)}$$

We define $freq(T)$ as the number of sentence pairs whose target sentence contains occurrences of all $t_i \in T$, and $freq(s_1)$ accordingly. The observation frequency $freq(s_1 \wedge T)$ is the number of sentence pairs that where s_1 occurs in the source sentence, and T in the target sentence.

The output translation can then be represented as a dependency configuration of the following kind *:((of,PMOD,%), (risk,NMOD,of),(risk,NMOD,the), (run,OBJ,risk), (run,SBJ,%))* which is the syntactic representation for the English MWE *run the risk of*.

3.3 Evaluation

Our translational approach to MWE extraction bears the advantage that evaluation is not exclusively bound to the manual judgement of candidate lists. Instead, we can first evaluate the system output against translation gold standards which are easier to obtain. The linguistic classification of the candidates according to their compositionality can then be treated as a separate problem.

We present two experiments in this evaluation section: We will first evaluate the translation detection on our gold standard to assess the general quality of the extraction method. Since this gold standard is to small to draw conclusions about the quality of MWE patterns that the system detects, we further evaluate the translational correspondences for a larger set of verbs.

Translation evaluation: In the first experiment, we extracted all types of translational correspondences for the verbs we annotated in the gold standard. We converted the output dependency configurations to the lemmatized bag-of-word form we already applied for the alignment evaluation and calculated the FPR and FNR of the translation types. The evaluation is displayed in table 4. Nearly all translation types that our system detected are correct. This confirms our hypothesis that syntactic filtering yields more reliable translations that just coocurrence-based alignments. However, the false negative rate is also very high. This low recall is due to the fact that our syntactic filters are very restrictive such that a major part of the occurrences of the source lemma don't figure in the prototypical syntactic configuration. Column two and three of the evaluation table present the FPR and FNR for experiments with a relaxed syntactic filter that doesn't constrain the syntactic type of the parallel argument relations. While not decreasing the FNR, the FPR decreases significantly. This means that the syntactic filters mainly fire on noisy configurations and don't decrease the recall. A manual error analysis has also shown that the relatively flat annotation scheme of our dependency parses significantly narrows down the number of candidate configurations that our algorithm detects. As the dependency parses don't provide deep analyses for tense or control phenomena, very often, a verb's arguments don't figure as its syntactic dependents and no configuration is found. Future work will explore the impact of deep syntactic analysis for the detection of translational correspondences.

MWE evaluation: In a second experiment, we evaluated the patterns of correspondences found by our extraction method for use in an MWE context. Therefore, we selected 50 random verbs occurring in the Europarl corpus and extracted their respective translational correspondences. This set of 50 verbs yields a set of 1592 one-to-many types of translational correspondences. We filtered the types wich display only morphological variation, such that the set of potential MWE types comprises 1302 types. Out of these, we evaluated a random sample of 300 types by labelling the types with the MWE categories we established for the analysis of our gold standard. During the classification, we encountered a further category of oneto- many correspondence which cannot be considered an MWE, the category of alternation. For instance, we found a translational correspondence between the active realization of the German verb *begrüßen* (en. *appreciate*) and the English passive *be pleased by*.

The classification is displayed in table 5. Almost 83% of the translational correspondences that our system extracted are perfect translation types. Almost 60% of the extracted types can be considered MWEs that exhibit some kind of semantic idiosyncrasy. The other translations could be classified as paraphrases or alternations. In our random sample, the portions of idioms is significantly higher than in our gold standard which confirms our intuition that the MWE pattern of the one-to-many translations for a given verb are related to language-specific, semantic properties of the verbs and the lexical concepts they realize.

4 Related Work

The problem sketched in this paper has clear conncetions to statistical MT. So-called phrase-based translation models generally target whole sentence alignment and do not necessarily recur to linguistically motivated phrase correspondences (Koehn et al., 2003). Syntax-based translation that specifies formal relations between bilingual parses was established by (Wu, 1997). Our way to use syntactic configurations can be seen as a heuristic to check relaxed structural parallelism.

	Strict Filter		Relaxed Filter	
	FPR	FNR	FPR	FNR
v_1	0.0	0.96	0.5	0.96
v_2	0.25	0.88	0.47	0.79
v_3	0.25	0.74	0.56	0.63
v_4	0.0	0.875	0.56	0.84

Table 4: False positive and false negative rate of one-to-many translations.

Trans. type	Proportion	MWE type	Proportion
MWEs	57.5%	V Part	8.2%
		V Prep	51.8%
		LVC	32.4%
		Idiom	10.6%
Paraphrases	24.4%		
Alternations	1.0%		
Noise	17.1%		

Table 5: Classification of 300 types sampled from the set of one-to-many translations for 50 verbs

Work on MWEs in a crosslingual context has almost exclusively focussed on MWE translation (Smadja and McKeown, 1994; Anastasiou, 2008). In (Villada Moirón and Tiedemann, 2006), the authors make use of alignment information in a parallel corpus to rank MWE candidates. These approaches don't rely on the lexical semantic knowledge about MWEs in form of one-to-many translations.

By contrast, previous approaches to paraphrase extraction made more explicit use of crosslingual semantic information. In (Bannard and Callison-Burch, 2005), the authors use the target language as a pivot providing contextual features for identifying semantically similar expressions. Paraphrasing is however only partially comparable to the crosslingual MWE detection we propose in this paper. Recently, the very pronounced context dependence of monolingual pairs of semantically similar expressions has been recognized as a major challenge in modelling word meaning (Erk and Pado, 2009).

The idea that parallel corpora can be used as a linguistic resource that provides empirical evidence for monolingual idiosyncrasies has already been exploited in, e.g. morphology projection (Yarowsky et al., 2001) or word sense disambiguation (Dyvik, 2004). While in a monolingual setting, it is quite tricky to come up with theoretical or empirical definitions of sense discriminations, the crosslingual scenario offers a theory-neutral, data-driven solution: Since ambiguity is an idiosyncratic property of a lexical item in a given language, it is not likely to be mirrored in a target language. Similarly, our approach can also be seen as a projection idea: we project the semantic information of simplex realization in a source language to an idiosyncratic, multiword realization in the target language.

5 Conclusion

We have explored the phenomenon of one-to-many translations in parallel corpora from the perspective of MWE identification. Our manual study on a translation gold standard as well as our experiments in automatic translation extraction have shown that one-to-many correspondences provide a rich resource and fruitful basis of study for data-driven MWE identification. The crosslingual perspective raises new research questions about the identification and interpretation of MWEs. It challenges the distinction between paraphrases and MWEs, a problem that does not arise at all in the context of monolingual MWE extraction. It also allows for the study of the relation between the semantics of lexical concepts and their MWE realization. Further research in this direction should investigate translational correspondences on a larger scale and further explore these for monolingual interpretation of MWEs.

Our extraction method that is based on syntactic filters identifies MWE types with a much higher precision than purely cooccurence-based word alignment and captures the various patterns we found in our gold standard. Future work on the extraction method will have to focus on the generalization of these filters and the generalization to other items than verbs. The experiments presented in this paper also suggest that the MWE realization of certain lexical items in a target language is subject to certain linguistic patterns. Moreover, the method we propose is completely languageindependent such that further research has to study the impact of the relatedness of the considered languages on the patterns of one-to-many translational correspondences.

References

Dimitra Anastasiou. 2008. Identification of idioms by mt's hybrid research system vs. three commercial system. In *Proceedings of the EAMT*, pp. 12–20.

Timothy Baldwin and Aline Villavicencio. 2002. Extracting the unextractable: a case study on verb-particles. In *Proceedings of the COLING-02*, pp. 1–7.

Colin Bannard and Chris Callison-Burch. 2005. Paraphrasing with bilingual parallel corpora. In *Proceedings of the 43rd Annual Meeting of the ACL*, pp. 597–604 .

Lea Cyrus. 2006. Building a resource for studying translation shifts. In *Proceedings of the 5th LREC*, pp. 1240–1245.

Helge Dyvik. 2004. Translations as semantic mirrors. From parallel corpus to WordNet. *Language and Computers*, 1:311 – 326.

Katrin Erk and Sebastian Pado. 2009. Paraphrase assessment in structured vector space: Exploring parameters and datasets. In *Proc. of the EACL GEMS Workshop*, pp. 57–65.

João de Almeida Varelas Graça, Joana Paulo Pardal, Luísa Coheur, and Diamantino António Caseiro. 2008. Multi-language word alignments annotation guidelines. Technical report, Tech. Rep. 38 / 2008 INESC-ID Lisboa.

Philipp Koehn, Franz Josef Och, and Daniel Marcu. 2003. Statistical phrase-based translation. In *Proceedings of the NAACL '03*, pp. 48–54.

Philipp Koehn. 2005. Europarl: A parallel corpus for statistical machine translation. In *MT Summit 2005*, pp. 79–86.

Joakim Nivre, Johan Hall, and Jens Nilsson. 2006. Malt-parser: A data driven parser-generator for dependency parsing. In *Proc. of LREC-2006*, pp. 2216–2219.

Franz Josef Och and Hermann Ney. 2003. A systematic comparison of various statistical alignment models. *Computational Linguistics*, 29(1):19–51.

Pavel Pecina. 2008. A machine learning approach to multi-word expression extraction. In *Proceedings of the LREC MWE 2008 Workshop*, pp. 54–57.

Ivan A. Sag, Timothy Baldwin, Francis Bond, and Ann Copestake. 2002. Multiword expressions: A pain in the neck for NLP. In *Proc. of the CICLing-2002*, pp. 1–15.

Frank Smadja and Kathleen McKeown. 1994. Translating collocations for use in bilingual lexicons. In *Proceedings of the HLT '94 workshop*, pp. 152–156.

Begoña Villada Moirón and Jörg Tiedemann. 2006. Identifying idiomatic expressions using automatic word-alignment. In *Proc. of the EACL MWE 2006 Workshop*, pp. 33–40.

Dekai Wu. 1997. Stochastic inversion transduction grammars and bilingual parsing of parallel corpora. *Comput. Linguist.*, 23(3):377–403.

David Yarowsky, Grace Ngai, and Richard Wicentowski. 2001. Inducing multilingual text analysis tools via robust projection across aligned corpora. In *Proceedings of HLT 2001*, pp. 1–8.

A Re-examination of Lexical Association Measures

Hung Huu Hoang
Dept. of Computer Science
National University of Singapore
hoanghuu@comp.nus.edu.sg

Su Nam Kim
Dept. of Computer Science and Software Engineering
University of Melbourne
snkim@csse.unimelb.edu.au

Min-Yen Kan
Dept. of Computer Science
National University of Singapore
kanmy@comp.nus.edu.sg

Abstract

We review lexical Association Measures (AMs) that have been employed by past work in extracting multiword expressions. Our work contributes to the understanding of these AMs by categorizing them into two groups and suggesting the use of rank equivalence to group AMs with the same ranking performance. We also examine how existing AMs can be adapted to better rank English verb particle constructions and light verb constructions. Specifically, we suggest normalizing (Pointwise) Mutual Information and using marginal frequencies to construct penalization terms. We empirically validate the effectiveness of these modified AMs in detection tasks in English, performed on the Penn Treebank, which shows significant improvement over the original AMs.

1 Introduction

Recently, the NLP community has witnessed a renewed interest in the use of lexical association measures in extracting Multiword Expressions (MWEs). Lexical Association Measures (hereafter, AMs) are mathematical formulas which can be used to capture the degree of connection or association between constituents of a given phrase. Well-known AMs include *Pointwise Mutual Information (PMI)*, *Pearson's* χ^2 and the *Odds Ratio*. These AMs have been applied in many different fields of study, from information retrieval to hypothesis testing. In the context of MWE extraction, many published works have been devoted to comparing their effectiveness. Krenn and Evert (2001) evaluate *Mutual Information (MI)*, *Dice*, *Pearson's* χ^2, *log-likelihood ratio* and the *T score*. In Pearce (2002), AMs such as *Z score*, *Pointwise MI*, *cost reduction*, *left and right context entropy*, *odds ratio* are evaluated. Evert (2004) discussed a wide range of AMs, including exact hypothesis tests such as *the binomial test* and *Fisher's exact test*s, various coefficients such as *Dice* and *Jaccard*. Later, Ramisch *et al.* (2008) evaluated *MI*, *Pearson's* χ^2 and *Permutation Entropy*. Probably the most comprehensive evaluation of AMs was presented in Pecina and Schlesinger (2006), where 82 AMs were assembled and evaluated over Czech collocations. These collocations contained a mix of idiomatic expressions, technical terms, light verb constructions and stock phrases. In their work, the best combination of AMs was selected using machine learning.

While the previous works have evaluated AMs, there have been few details on why the AMs perform as they do. A detailed analysis of why these AMs perform as they do is needed in order to explain their identification performance, and to help us recommend AMs for future tasks. This weakness of previous works motivated us to address this issue. In this work, we contribute to further understanding of association measures, using two different MWE extraction tasks to motivate and concretize our discussion. Our goal is to be able to predict, *a priori*, what types of AMs are likely to perform well for a particular MWE class.

We focus on the extraction of two common types of English MWEs that can be captured by bigram model: Verb Particle Constructions (VPCs) and Light Verb Constructions (LVCs). VPCs consist of a verb and one or more particles, which can be prepositions (e.g. *put on*, *bolster up*), adjectives (*cut short*) or verbs (*make do*). For simplicity, we focus only on bigram VPCs that take prepositional particles, the most common class of VPCs. A special characteristic of VPCs that affects their extraction is the

Proceedings of the 2009 Workshop on Multiword Expressions, ACL-IJCNLP 2009, pages 31–39,
Suntec, Singapore, 6 August 2009. ©2009 ACL and AFNLP

mobility of noun phrase complements in transitive VPCs. They can appear after the particle (*Take off your hat*) or between the verb and the particle (*Take your hat off*). However, a pronominal complement can only appear in the latter configuration (*Take it off*).

In comparison, LVCs comprise of a verb and a complement, which is usually a noun phrase (*make a presentation*, *give a demonstration*). Their meanings come mostly from their complements and, as such, verbs in LVCs are termed semantically light, hence the name *light verb*. This explains why modifiers of LVCs modify the complement instead of the verb (*make a serious mistake* vs. *make a mistake seriously*). This phenomenon also shows that an LVC's constituents may not occur contiguously.

2 Classification of Association Measures

Although different AMs have different approaches to measuring association, we observed that they can effectively be classified into two broad classes. *Class I* AMs look at the degree of institutionalization; i.e., the extent to which the phrase is a semantic unit rather than a free combination of words. Some of the AMs in this class directly measure this association between constituents using various combinations of co-occurrence and marginal frequencies. Examples include *MI*, *PMI* and their variants as well as most of the association coefficients such as *Jaccard*, *Hamann*, *Brawn-Blanquet*, and others. Other Class I AMs estimate a phrase's MWE-hood by judging the significance of the difference between observed and expected frequencies. These AMs include, among others, statistical hypothesis tests such as *T score*, *Z score* and *Pearson's* χ^2 *test*.

Class II AMs feature the use of context to measure non-compositionality, a peculiar characteristic of many types of MWEs, including VPCs and idioms. This is commonly done in one of the following two ways. First, non-compositionality can be modeled through the diversity of contexts, measured using entropy. The underlying assumption of this approach is that non-compositional phrases appear in a more restricted set of contexts than compositional ones. Second, non-compositionality can also be measured through context similarity between the phrase and its constituents. The observation here is that non-compositional phrases have different semantics from those of their constituents. It then follows that contexts in which the phrase and its constituents appear would be different (Zhai, 1997). Some VPC examples include *carry out*, *give up*. A close approximation stipulates that contexts of a non-compositional phrase's constituents are also different. For instance, phrases such as *hot dog* and *Dutch courage* are comprised of constituents that have unrelated meanings. Metrics that are commonly used to compute context similarity include *cosine* and *dice similarity*; distance metrics such as *Euclidean* and *Manhattan norm*; and probability distribution measures such as *Kullback-Leibler divergence* and *Jensen-Shannon divergence*.

Table 1 lists all AMs used in our discussion. The lower left legend defines the variables *a, b, c*, and *d* with respect to the raw co-occurrence statistics observed in the corpus data. When an AM is introduced, it is prefixed with its index given in Table 1(e.g., [M2] Mutual Information) for the reader's convenience.

3 Evaluation

We will first present how VPC and LVC candidates are extracted and used to form our evaluation data set. Second, we will discuss how performances of AMs are measured in our experiments.

3.1 Evaluation Data

In this study, we employ the *Wall Street Journal* (WSJ) section of one million words in the Penn Tree Bank. To create the evaluation data set, we first extract the VPC and LVC candidates from our corpus as described below. We note here that the mobility property of both VPC and LVC constituents have been used in the extraction process.

For VPCs, we first identify particles using a pre-compiled set of 38 particles based on Baldwin (2005) and Quirk *et al.* (1985) (Appendix A). Here we do not use the WSJ particle tag to avoid possible inconsistencies pointed out in Baldwin (2005). Next, we search to the left of the located particle for the nearest verb. As verbs and particles in transitive VPCs may not occur contiguously, we allow an intervening NP of up to 5 words, similar to Baldwin and Villavicencio (2002) and Smadja (1993), since longer NPs tend to be located after particles.

AM Name	Formula	AM Name	Formula
M1. Joint Probability	$f(xy)/N$	M2. Mutual Information	$\frac{1}{N}\sum_{i,j} f_{ij}\log\frac{f_{ij}}{\hat{f}_{ij}}$
M3. Log likelihood ratio	$2\sum_{i,j} f_{ij}\log\frac{f_{ij}}{\hat{f}_{ij}}$	M4. Pointwise MI (PMI)	$\log\frac{P(xy)}{P(x*)P(*y)}$
M5. Local-PMI	$f(xy)\times \text{PMI}$	M6. PMI^k	$\log\frac{Nf(xy)^k}{f(x*)f(*y)}$
M7. PMI^2	$\log\frac{Nf(xy)^2}{f(x*)f(*y)}$	M8. Mutual Dependency	$\log\frac{P(xy)^2}{P(x*)P(*y)}$
M9. Driver-Kroeber	$\frac{a}{\sqrt{(a+b)(a+c)}}$	M10. Normalized expectation	$\frac{2a}{2a+b+c}$
M11. Jaccard	$\frac{a}{a+b+c}$	M12. First Kulczynski	$\frac{a}{b+c}$
M13. Second Sokal-Sneath	$\frac{a}{a+2(b+c)}$	M14. Third Sokal-Sneath	$\frac{a+d}{b+c}$
M15. Sokal-Michiner	$\frac{a+d}{a+b+c+d}$	M16. Rogers-Tanimoto	$\frac{a+d}{a+2b+2c+d}$
M17. Hamann	$\frac{(a+d)-(b+c)}{a+b+c+d}$	M18. Odds ratio	$\frac{ad}{bc}$
M19. Yule's ω	$\frac{\sqrt{ad}-\sqrt{bc}}{\sqrt{ad}+\sqrt{bc}}$	M20. Yule's Q	$\frac{ad-bc}{ad+bc}$
M21. Brawn-Blanquet	$\frac{a}{\max(a+b, a+c)}$	M22. Simpson	$\frac{a}{\min(a+b, a+c)}$
M23. S cost	$\log(1+\frac{\min(b,c)}{a+1})^{-\frac{1}{2}}$	M24*. Adjusted S Cost	$\log(1+\frac{\max(b,c)}{a+1})^{-\frac{1}{2}}$
M25. Laplace	$\frac{a+1}{a+\min(b, c)+2}$	M26*. Adjusted Laplace	$\frac{a+1}{a+\max(b, c)+2}$
M27. Fager	$[\text{M9}]-\frac{1}{2}\max(b,c)$	M28*. Adjusted Fager	$[\text{M9}]-\frac{1}{\sqrt{aN}}\max(b,c)$
M29*. Normalized PMIs	PMI / NF(α) PMI / NFMax	M30*. Simplified normalized PMI for VPCs	$\frac{\log(ad)}{\alpha\times b+(1-\alpha)\times c}$
M31*. Normalized MIs	MI / NF(α) MI / NFMax	$\text{NF}(\alpha) = \alpha P(x*) + (1-\alpha)P(*y) \quad \alpha\in[0, 1]$ $\text{NFMax} = \max(P(x*), P(*y))$	

$a = f_{11} = f(xy)$	$b = f_{12} = f(x\bar{y})$	$f(x*)$
$c = f_{21} = f(\bar{x}y)$	$d = f_{22} = f(\bar{x}\bar{y})$	$f(\bar{x}*)$
$f(*y)$	$f(*\bar{y})$	N

Contingency table of a bigram (x y), recording co-occurrence and marginal frequencies; $\bar{w}$ stands for all words except w; * stands for all words; N is total number of bigrams. The expected frequency under the independence assumption is $\hat{f}(xy) = f(x*)f(*y)/N$.

Table 1. Association measures discussed in this paper. Starred AMs (*) are developed in this work.

Extraction of LVCs is carried out in a similar fashion. First, occurrences of light verbs are located based on the following set of seven frequently used English light verbs: *do*, *get*, *give*, *have*, *make*, *put* and *take*. Next, we search to the right of the light verbs for the nearest noun, permitting a maximum of 4 intervening words to allow for quantifiers (*a/an*, *the*, *many*, etc.), adjectival and adverbial modifiers, etc. If this search fails to find a noun, as when LVCs are used in the passive (e.g. *the presentation was made*), we search to the right of the light verb, also allowing a maximum of 4 intervening words. The above extraction process produced a total of 8,652 VPC and 11,465 LVC candidates when run on the corpus. We then filter out candidates with observed frequencies less than 6, as suggested in Pecina and Schlesinger (2006), to obtain a set of 1,629 VPCs and 1,254 LVCs.

Separately, we use the following two available sources of annotations: 3,078 VPC candidates extracted and annotated in (Baldwin, 2005) and 464 annotated LVC candidates used in (Tan *et al.*, 2006). Both sets of annotations give both positive and negative examples.

Our final VPC and LVC evaluation datasets were then constructed by intersecting the gold-standard datasets with our corresponding sets of extracted candidates. We also concatenated both sets of evaluation data for composite evaluation. This set is referred to as "Mixed". Statistics of our three evaluation datasets are summarized in Table 2.

	VPC data	LVC data	Mixed
Total (*freq* ≥ 6)	413	100	513
Positive instances	117 (28.33%)	28 (28%)	145 (23.26%)

Table 2. Evaluation data sizes (type count, not token).

While these datasets are small, our primary goal in this work is to establish initial comparable baselines and describe interesting phenomena that we plan to investigate over larger datasets in future work.

3.2 Evaluation Metric

To evaluate the performance of AMs, we can use the standard precision and recall measures, as in much past work. We note that the ranked list of candidates generated by an AM is often used as a classifier by setting a threshold. However, setting a threshold is problematic and optimal threshold values vary for different AMs. Additionally, using the list of ranked candidates directly as a classifier does not consider the confidence indicated by actual scores. Another way to avoid setting threshold values is to measure precision and recall of only the n most likely candidates (the n-best method). However, as discussed in Evert and Krenn (2001), this method depends heavily on the choice of n. In this paper, we opt for average precision (AP), which is the average of precisions at all possible recall values. This choice also makes our results comparable to those of Pecina and Schlesinger (2006).

3.3 Evaluation Results

Figure 1(a, b) gives the two average precision profiles of the 82 AMs presented in Pecina and Schlesinger (2006) when we replicated their experiments over our English VPC and LVC datasets. We observe that the average precision profile for VPCs is slightly concave while the one for LVCs is more convex. This can be interpreted as VPCs being more sensitive to the choice of AM than LVCs. Another point we observed is that a vast majority of Class I AMs, including PMI, its variants and association coefficients (excluding hypothesis tests), perform reasonably well in our application. In contrast, the performances of most of context-based and hypothesis test AMs are very modest. Their mediocre performance indicates their inapplicability to our VPC and LVC tasks. In particular, the high frequencies of particles in VPCs and light verbs in LVCs both undermine their contexts' discriminative power and skew the difference between observed and expected frequencies that are relied on in hypothesis tests.

4 Rank Equivalence

We note that some AMs, although not mathematically equivalent (i.e., assigning identical scores to input candidates) produce the same lists of ranked candidates on our datasets. Hence, they achieve the same average precision. The ability to identify such groups of AMs is helpful in simplifying their formulas, which in turn assisting in analyzing their meanings.

Definition: *Association measures* M_1 *and* M_2 *are rank equivalent over a set C, denoted by* $M_1 \overset{r}{\underset{C}{\equiv}} M_2$, *if and only if* $M_1(c_j) > M_1(c_k) \Leftrightarrow M_2(c_j) > M_2(c_k)$ *and* $M_1(c_j) = M_1(c_k) \Leftrightarrow M_2(c_j) = M_2(c_k)$ *for all* c_j, c_k *belongs to C where* $M_k(c_i)$ *denotes the score assigned to* c_i *by the measure* M_k.

As a corollary, the following also holds for rank equivalent AMs:

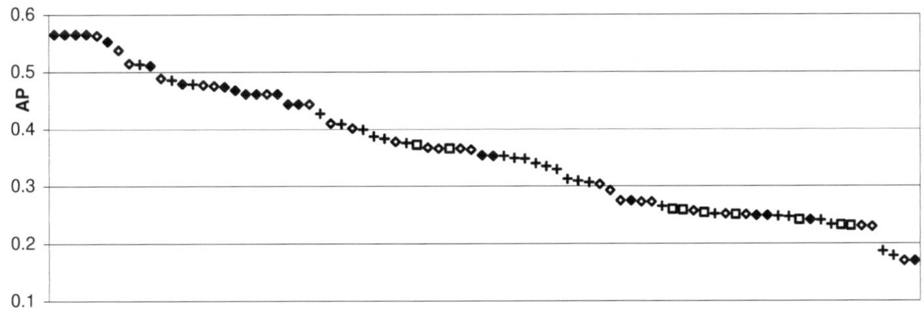

Figure 1a. AP profile of AMs examined over our VPC data set.

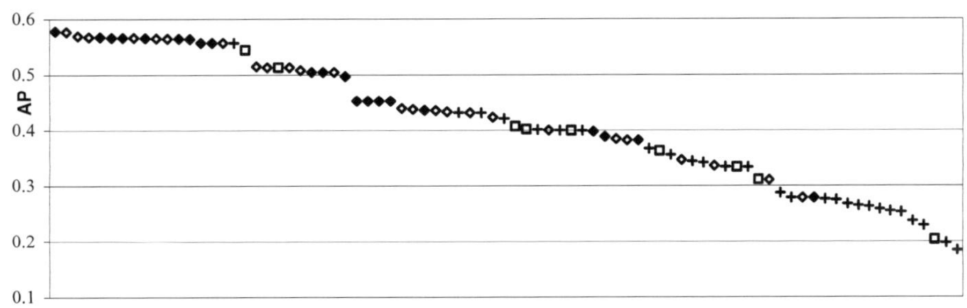

Figure 1b. AP profile of AMs examined over our LVC data set.

Figure 1. Average precision (AP) performance of the 82 AMs from Pecina and Schlesinger (2006), on our English VPC and LVC datasets. Bold points indicate AMs discussed in this paper.
□ Hypothesis test AMs ◊ Class I AMs, excluding hypothesis test AMs + Context-based AMs.

Corollary: *If* $M_1 \underset{C}{\overset{r}{\equiv}} M_2$ *then* $AP_C(M_1) = AP_C(M_2)$ *where* $AP_C(M_i)$ *stands for the average precision of the AM* M_i *over the data set C.*

Essentially, M_1 and M_2 are rank equivalent over a set C if their ranked lists of all candidates taken from C are the same, ignoring the actual calculated scores[1]. As an example, the following 3 AMs: *Odds ratio*, *Yule's ω* and *Yule's Q* (Table 3, row 5), though not mathematically equivalent, can be shown to be rank equivalent. Five groups of rank equivalent AMs that we have found are listed in Table 3. This allows us to replace the below 15 AMs with their (most simple) representatives from each rank equivalent group.

1) [M2] Mutual Information, [M3] Log likelihood ratio
2) [M7] PMI², [M8] Mutual Dependency, [M9] Driver-Kroeber (a.k.a. Ochiai)
3) [M10] Normalized expectation, [M11] Jaccard, [M12] First Kulczynski, [M13]Second Sokal-Sneath (a.k.a. Anderberg)
4) [M14] Third Sokal-Sneath, [M15] Sokal-Michiner, [M16] Rogers-Tanimoto, [M17] Hamann
5) [M18] Odds ratio, [M19] Yule's *ω*, [M20] Yule's Q

Table 3. Five groups of rank equivalent AMs.

5 Examination of Association Measures

We highlight two important findings in our analysis of the AMs over our English datasets. Section 5.1 focuses on MI and PMI and Section 5.2 discusses penalization terms.

5.1 Mutual Information and Pointwise Mutual Information

In Figure 1, over 82 AMs, PMI ranks 11th in identifying VPCs while MI ranks 35th in

[1] Two AMs may be rank equivalent with the exception of some candidates where one AM is undefined due to a zero in the denominator while the other AM is still well-defined. We call these cases *weakly rank equivalent*. With a reasonably large corpus, such candidates are rare for our VPC and LVC types. Hence, we still consider such AM pairs to be rank equivalent.

identifying LVCs. In this section, we show how their performances can be improved significantly.

Mutual Information (MI) measures the common information between two variables or the reduction in uncertainty of one variable given knowledge of the other. $\text{MI}(U; V) = \sum_{u,v} p(uv) \log \frac{p(uv)}{p(u*)p(*v)}$. In the context of bigrams, the above formula can be simplified to [M2] $\text{MI} = \frac{1}{N} \sum_{i,j} f_{ij} \log \frac{f_{ij}}{\hat{f}_{ij}}$. While MI holds between random variables, [M4] Pointwise MI (PMI) holds between specific values: $\text{PMI}(x, y) = \log \frac{P(xy)}{P(x*)P(*y)} = \log \frac{Nf(xy)}{f(x*)f(*y)}$. It has long been pointed out that PMI favors bigrams with low-frequency constituents, as evidenced by the product of two marginal frequencies in its denominator. To reduce this bias, a common solution is to assign more weight to the co-occurrence frequency $f(xy)$ in the numerator by either raising it to some power k (Daille, 1994) or multiplying PMI with $f(xy)$. Table 4 lists these adjusted versions of PMI and their performance over our datasets. We can see from Table 4 that the best performance of PMI^k is obtained at k values less than one, indicating that it is better to rely less on $f(xy)$. Similarly, multiplying $f(xy)$ directly to PMI reduces the performance of PMI. As such, assigning more weight to $f(xy)$ does not improve the AP performance of PMI.

AM	VPCs	LVCs	Mixed
Best [M6] PMI^k	.547 (k = .13)	.573 (k = .85)	.544 (k = .32)
[M4] PMI	.510	.566	.515
[M5] Local-PMI	.259	.393	.272
[M1] Joint Prob.	.170	.28	.175

Table 4. AP performance of PMI and its variants. Best alpha settings shown in parentheses.

Another shortcoming of (P)MI is that both grow not only with the degree of dependence but also with frequency (Manning and Schütze, 1999, p. 66). In particular, we can show that $\text{MI}(X; Y) \leq \min(H(X), H(Y))$, where $H(.)$ denotes entropy, and $\text{PMI}(x,y) \leq \min(-\log P(x*), -\log P(*y))$.

These two inequalities suggest that the allowed score ranges of different candidates vary and consequently, MI and PMI scores are not directly comparable. Furthermore, in the case of VPCs and LVCs, the differences among score ranges of different candidates are large, due to high frequencies of particles and light verbs. This has motivated us to normalize these scores before using them for comparison. We suggest MI and PMI be divided by one of the following two normalization factors: $\text{NF}(\alpha) = \alpha P(x*) + (1-\alpha)P(*y)$ with $\alpha \in [0, 1]$ and NFmax $= \max(P(x*), P(*y))$. $\text{NF}(\alpha)$, being dependent on alpha, can be optimized by setting an appropriate alpha value, which is inevitably affected by the MWE type and the corpus statistics. On the other hand, NFmax is independent of alpha and is recommended when one needs to apply normalized (P)MI to a mixed set of different MWE types or when sufficient data for parameter tuning is unavailable. As shown in Table 5, normalized MI and PMI show considerable improvements of up to 80%. Also, PMI and MI, after being normalized with NFmax, rank number one in VPC and LVC task, respectively. If one re-writes MI as $= (1/N) \sum_{i,j} f_{ij} \times \text{PMI}_{ij}$, it is easy to see the heavy dependence of MI on direct frequencies compared with PMI and this explains why normalization is a pressing need for MI.

AM	VPCs	LVCs	Mixed
MI / $\text{NF}(\alpha)$	.508 (α = .48)	.583 (α = .47)	.516 (α = .5)
MI / NFmax	.508	.584	.518
[M2] MI	.273	.435	.289
PMI / $\text{NF}(\alpha)$	.592 (α = .8)	.554 (α = .48)	.588 (α = .77)
PMI / NFmax	.565	.517	.556
[M4] PMI	.510	.566	.515

Table 5. AP performance of normalized (P)MI versus standard (P)MI. Best alpha settings shown in parentheses.

5.2 Penalization Terms

It can be seen that given equal co-occurrence frequencies, higher marginal frequencies reduce the likelihood of being MWEs. This motivates us to use marginal frequencies to synthesize *penalization terms* which are formulae whose values are inversely proportional to the likelihood of being MWEs. We hypothesize that incorporating such penalization terms can improve the respective AMs detection AP.

Take as an example, the AMs *[M21] Brawn-Blanquet* (a.k.a. *Minimum Sensitivity*) and *[M22] Simpson*. These two AMs are identical, except for one difference in the denominator: *Brawn-Blanquet* uses max(*b, c*); *Simpson* uses min(*b, c*). It is intuitive and confirmed by our experiments that penalizing against the more frequent constituent by choosing max(*b, c*) is more effective. This is further attested in AMs *[M23] S Cost* and *[M25] Laplace*, where we tried to replace the min(*b, c*) term with max(*b, c*). Table 6 shows the average precision on our datasets for all these AMs.

AM	VPCs	LVCs	Mixed
[M21]Brawn-Blanquet	.478	.578	.486
[M22] Simpson	.249	.382	.260
[M24] Adjusted S Cost	.485	.577	.492
[M23] S cost	.249	.388	.260
[M26] Adjusted Laplace	.486	.577	.493
[M25] Laplace	.241	.388	.254

Table 6. Replacing *min*() with *max*() in selected AMs.

In the *[M27] Fager* AM, the penalization term max(*b, c*) is subtracted from the first term, which is no stranger but rank equivalent to [M7] PMI^2. In our application, this AM is not good since the second term is far larger than the first term, which is less than 1. As such, *Fager* is largely equivalent to just –½ max(*b, c*). In order to make use of the first term, we need to replace the constant ½ by a scaled down version of max(*b, c*). We have approximately derived $1/\sqrt{aN}$ as a lower bound estimate of max(*b, c*) using the independence assumption, producing *[M28] Adjusted Fager*. We can see from Table 7 that this adjustment improves Fager on both datasets.

AM	VPCs	LVCs	Mixed
[M28] Adjusted Fager	.564	.543	.554
[M27] Fager	.552	.439	.525

Table 7. Performance of *Fager* and its adjusted version.

The next experiment involves *[M14] Third Sokal Sneath*, which can be shown to be rank equivalent to *–b –c*. We further notice that frequencies *c* of particles are normally much larger than frequencies *b* of verbs. Thus, this AM runs the risk of ranking VPC candidates based on only frequencies of particles. So, it is necessary that we scale *b* and *c* properly as in [M14'] $-\alpha \times b - (1-\alpha)\times c$. Having scaled the constituents properly, we still see that [M14'] by itself is not a good measure as it uses only constituent frequencies and does not take into consideration the co-occurrence frequency of the two constituents. This has led us to experiment with [MR14"] $\dfrac{\mathrm{PMI}}{\alpha \times b + (1-\alpha)\times c}$. The denominator of [MR14"] is obtained by removing the minus sign from [MR14'] so that it can be used as a penalization term. The choice of PMI in the numerator is due to the fact that the denominator of [MR14"] is in essence similar to $\mathrm{NF}(\alpha) = \alpha P(x*) + (1-\alpha)P(*y)$, which has been successfully used to divide PMI in the normalized PMI experiment. We heuristically tried to simplify [MR14"] to the following AM [M30] $\dfrac{\log(ad)}{\alpha \times b + (1-\alpha)\times c}$. The setting of alpha in Table 8 below is taken from the best alpha setting obtained the experiment on the normalized PMI (Table 5). It can be observed from Table 8 that [MR14'"], being computationally simpler than normalized PMI, performs as well as normalized PMI and better than *Third Sokal-Sneath* over the VPC data set.

AM	VPCs	LVCs	Mixed
PMI / NF(α)	.592 (α=.8)	.554 (α=.48)	.588 (α=.77)
[M30] $\dfrac{\log(ad)}{\alpha \times b + (1-\alpha)\times c}$	.600 (α=.8)	.484 (α=.48)	.588 (α=.77)
[M14] Third Sokal Sneath	.565	.453	.546

Table 8. AP performance of suggested VPCs' penalization terms and AMs.

With the same intention and method, we have found that while addition of marginal frequencies is a good penalization term for VPCs, the product of marginal frequencies is more suitable for LVCs (rows 1 and 2, Table 9). As with the linear combination, the product *bc* should also be weighted accordingly as $b^{\alpha}c^{(1-\alpha)}$. The best alpha value is also taken from the normalized PMI experiments (Table 5), which is nearly .5. Under this setting, this penalization term is exactly the denominator of the *[M18] Odds Ratio*. Table 9 below show our experiment results in deriving the penalization term for LVCs.

AM	VPCs	LVCs	Mixed
–b –c	.565	.453	.546
1/bc	.502	.532	.502
[M18] Odds ratio	.443	.567	.456

Table 9. AP performance of suggested LVCs' penalization terms and AMs.

6 Conclusions

We have conducted an analysis of the 82 AMs assembled in Pecina and Schlesinger (2006) for the tasks of English VPC and LVC extraction over the *Wall Street Journal* Penn Treebank data. In our work, we have observed that AMs can be divided into two classes: ones that do not use context (Class I) and ones that do (Class II), and find that the latter is not suitable for our VPC and LVC detection tasks as the size of our corpus is too small to rely on the frequency of candidates' contexts. This phenomenon also revealed the inappropriateness of hypothesis tests for our detection task. We have also introduced the novel notion of rank equivalence to MWE detection, in which we show that complex AMs may be replaced by simpler AMs that yield the same average precision performance.

We further observed that certain modifications to some AMs are necessary. First, in the context of ranking, we have proposed normalizing scores produced by MI and PMI in cases where the distributions of the two events are markedly different, as is the case for light verbs and particles. While our claims are limited to the datasets analyzed, they show clear improvements: normalized PMI produces better performance over our mixed MWE dataset, yielding an average precision of 58.8% compared to 51.5% when using standard PMI, a significant improvement as judged by paired T test. Normalized MI also yields the best performance over our LVC dataset with a significantly improved AP of 58.3%.

We also show that marginal frequencies can be used to form effective penalization terms. In particular, we find that $\alpha \times b + (1-\alpha) \times c$ is a good penalization term for VPCs, while $b^{\alpha}c^{(1-\alpha)}$ is suitable for LVCs. Our introduced alpha tuning parameter should be set to properly scale the values *b* and *c,* and should be optimized per MWE type. In cases where a common factor is applied to different MWE types, max(*b, c*) is a better choice than min(*b, c*). In future work, we plan to expand our investigations over larger, web-based datasets of English, to verify the performance gains of our modified AMs.

Acknowledgement

This work was partially supported by a National Research Foundation grant "Interactive Media Search" (grant # R 252 000 325 279).

References

Baldwin, Timothy (2005). The deep lexical acquisition of English verb-particle constructions. *Computer Speech and Language, Special Issue on Multiword Expressions*, 19(4):398–414.

Baldwin, Timothy and Villavicencio, Aline (2002). Extracting the unextractable: A case study on verb-particles. In *Proceedings of the 6th Conference on Natural Language Learning (CoNLL-2002)*, pages 98–104, Taipei, Taiwan.

Daille, Béatrice (1994). *Approche mixte pour l'extraction automatique de terminologie: statistiques lexicales et filtres linguistiques.* PhD thesis, Université Paris 7.

Evert, Stefan (2004). Online repository of association measures http://www.collocations.de/, a companion to *The Statistics of Word Cooccurrences: Word Pairs and Collocations.* Ph.D. dissertation, University of Stuttgart.

Evert, Stefan and Krenn, Brigitte (2001) Methods for qualitative evaluation of lexical association measures. In *Proceedings of the 39th Annual Meeting of the Association of Computational Linguistics,* pages 188-915, Toulouse, France.

Katz, Graham and Giesbrecht, Eugenie (2006). Automatic identification of non-compositional multi-word expressions using latent semantic analysis. In *Proceedings of the ACL Workshop on Multiword Expressions: Identifying and Exploiting Underlying Properties*, pages 12-19, Sydney, Australia.

Krenn, Brigitte and Evert, Stefan (2001). Can we do better than frequency? A case study on extracting PP-verb collocations. In *Proceedings of the ACL/EACL 2001 Workshop on the Computational Extraction, Analysis and Exploitation of Collocations*, pages 39–46, Toulouse, France.

Manning D. Christopher and Schütze, Hinrich (1999). *Foundations of Statistical Natural Language Processing.* The MIT Press, Cambridge, Massachusetts.

Pearce, Darren (2002). A comparative evaluation of collocation extraction techniques. In *Proc. of the*

3rd International Conference on Language Resources and Evaluation (LREC 2002), Las Palmas, pages 1530-1536, Canary Islands.

Pecina, Pavel and Schlesinger, Pavel (2006). Combining association measures for collocation extraction. In *Proceedings of the 21th International Conference on Computational Linguistics and 44th Annual Meeting of the Association for Computational Linguistics (COLING/ACL 2006)*, pages 651-658, Sydney, Australia.

Quirk Randolph, Greenbaum Sidney, Leech Geoffrey and Svartvik Jan (1985). *A Comprehensive Grammar of the English Language*. Longman, London, UK.

Ramisch Carlos, Schreiner Paulo, Idiart Marco and Villavicencio Aline (2008). An Evaluation of Methods for the extraction of Multiword Expressions. In *Proceedings of the LREC-2008 Workshop on Multiword Expressions: Towards a Shared Task for Multiword Expressions*, pages 50-53, Marrakech, Morocco.

Smadja, Frank (1993). Retrieving collocations from text: Xtract. *Computational Linguistics* 19(1): 143–77.

Tan, Y. Fan, Kan M. Yen and Cui, Hang (2006). Extending corpus-based identification of light verb constructions using a supervised learning framework. In *Proceedings of the EACL 2006 Workshop on Multi-word-expressions in a multilingual context*, pages 49–56, Trento, Italy.

Zhai, Chengxiang (1997). Exploiting context to identify lexical atoms – A statistical view of linguistic context. In *International and Interdisciplinary Conference on Modelling and Using Context (CONTEXT-97)*, pages 119-129, Rio de Janeiro, Brazil.

Appendix A. List of particles used in identifying verb particle constructions.

about, aback, aboard, above, abroad, across, adrift, ahead, along, apart, around, aside, astray, away, back, backward, backwards, behind, by, down, forth, forward, forwards, in, into, off, on, out, over, past, round, through, to, together, under, up, upon, without.

Mining Complex Predicates In Hindi Using A Parallel Hindi-English Corpus

R. Mahesh K. Sinha
Department of Computer Science & Engineering
Indian Institute of Technology, Kanpur
Kanpur 208016 India
rmk@iitk.ac.in

Abstract

Complex predicate is a noun, a verb, an adjective or an adverb followed by a light verb that behaves as a single unit of verb. Complex predicates (CPs) are abundantly used in Hindi and other languages of Indo Aryan family. Detecting and interpreting CPs constitute an important and somewhat a difficult task. The linguistic and statistical methods have yielded limited success in mining this data. In this paper, we present a simple method for detecting CPs of all kinds using a Hindi-English parallel corpus. A CP is hypothesized by detecting absence of the conventional meaning of the light verb in the aligned English sentence. This simple strategy exploits the fact that CP is a multiword expression with a meaning that is distinct from the meaning of the light verb. Although there are several shortcomings in the methodology, this empirical method surprisingly yields mining of CPs with an average precision of 89% and a recall of 90%.

1 Introduction

Complex predicates (CPs) are abundantly used in Hindi and other languages of Indo-Aryan family and have been widely studied (Hook, 1974; Abbi, 1992; Verma, 1993; Mohanan, 1994; Singh, 1994; Butt, 1995; Butt and Geuder, 2001; Butt and Ramchand, 2001; Butt et al., 2003). A complex predicate is a multi-word expression (MWE) where a noun, a verb or an adjective is followed by a light verb (LV) and the MWE behaves as a single unit of verb. The general theory of complex predicate is discussed in Alsina (1996). These studies attempt to model the linguistic facts of complex predicate formation and the associated semantic roles.

CPs empower the language in its expressiveness but are hard to detect. Detection and interpretation of CPs are important for several tasks of natural language processing tasks such as machine translation, information retrieval, summarization etc. A mere listing of the CPs constitutes a valuable linguistic resource for lexicographers, wordnet designers (Chakrabarti et al., 2007) and other NLP system designers. Computational method using Hindi corpus has been used to mine CPs and categorize them based on statistical analysis (Sriram and Joshi, 2005) with limited success. Chakrabarti et al. (2008) present a method for automatic extraction of V+V CPs only from a corpus based on linguistic features. They report an accuracy of about 98%. An attempt has also been made to use a parallel corpus for detecting CPs using projection POS tags from English to Hindi (Soni, Mukerjee and Raina, 2006). It uses Giza++ word alignment tool to align the projected POS information. A success of 83% precision and 46% recall has been reported.

In this paper, we present a simple strategy for mining of CPs in Hindi using projection of meaning of light verb in a parallel corpus. In the following section the nature of CP in Hindi is outlined and this is followed by system design, experimentation and results.

2 Complex Predicates in Hindi

A CP in Hindi is a syntactic construction consisting of either a verb, a noun, an adjective or an adverb as main predicator followed by a light verb (LV). Thus, a CP can be a noun+LV, an adjective+LV, a verb+LV or an adverb+LV. Further, it is also possible that a CP is followed by a LV (CP+LV). The light verb carries the tense and agreement morphology. In V+V CPs, the contribution of the light verb denotes aspectual terms such as continuity, perfectivity, inception, completion, or denotes an expression of forcefulness, suddenness, etc. (Singh, 1994; Butt, 1995). The CP in a sentence syntactically acts as a single lexical unit of verb that has a meaning dis-

Proceedings of the 2009 Workshop on Multiword Expressions, ACL-IJCNLP 2009, pages 40–46,
Suntec, Singapore, 6 August 2009.

tinct from that of the LV. CPs are also referred as the complex or compound verbs.

Given below are some examples:

(1): CP=noun+LV
noun = *ashirwad*_{blessings}
LV = *denaa* {to give}
usane mujhe ashirwad diyaa.
उसने मुझे आर्शीवाद दिया
{he me blessings gave}
he blessed me.

(2) No CP
usane mujhe ek pustak dii.
उसने मुझे एक पुस्तक दी
{he me one book gave}
he gave_me a book.

In (1), the light verb *diyaa* (gave) in its past tense form with the noun *ashirwad* (blessings) makes a complex predicate verb form *ashirwad diyaa* (blessed) in the past tense form. The CP here is *ashirwad denaa* and its corresponding English translation is 'to bless'. On the other hand in example (2), the verb *dii* (gave) is a simple verb in past tense form and is not a light verb. Although, same Hindi verb *denaa* (to give) is used in both the examples, it is a light verb in (1) and a main verb in (2). Whether it acts as a light verb or not, depends upon the semantics of the preceding noun. However, it is observed that the English meaning in case of the complex predicate is not derived from the individual meanings of the constituent words. It is this observation that forms basis of our approach for mining of CPs.

(3) CP=adjective+LV
adjective=khush {happy}
LV=*karanaa* {to do}
usane mujhe khush kiyaa.
उसने मुझे खुश किया
{he me happy did}
he pleased me.

Here the Hindi verb *kiyaa* (did) is the past tense form of a light verb *karanaa* (to do) and the preceding word *khush* (happy) is an adjective. The CP here is *khush karanaa* (to please).

(4) CP=verb+LV
verb = *paRhnaa*_{to read}
LV = *lenaa*_{to take}
usane pustak paRh liyaa.
उसने पुस्तक पढ़ लिया
{he book read took}
he has read the book.

Here the Hindi verb *liyaa* (took) is the past tense form of the light verb *lenaa* (to take) and the preceding word *paRh* (read) is the verb *paRhnaa* (to read) in its stem form. The CP is *paRh lenaa* (to finish reading). In such cases the light verb acts as an aspectual /modal or as an intensifier.

(5) CP=verb+LV
verb = *phaadanaa*_{to tear}
LV = *denaa*_{to give}
usane pustak phaad diyaa.
उसने पुस्तक फाड़ दिया
{he book tear gave}
he has torn the book.

Here the Hindi verb *diyaa* (gave) is the past tense form of the light verb *denaa*_(to give) and the preceding word *phaad* (tear) is the stem form of the verb *phaadanaa*_(to tear) . The CP is *phaad denaa* (to cause and complete act of tearing).

(6) CP=verb+LV
verb = *denaa*_{to give}
LV = *maaranaa*{to hit/ to kill}
usane pustak de maaraa.
उसने पुस्तक दे मारा
{he book give hit}
he threw the book.

Here the Hindi verb *maaraa* (hit/killed) is the past tense form of the light verb *maaranaa* (to hit/ to kill) and the preceding word *de* (give) is a verb *denaa* (to give) in its stem form. The CP is *de maranaa* (to throw). The verb combination yields a new meaning. This may also be considered as a semi-idiomatic construct by some people.

(7) CP=adverb+LV1+LV2
adverb = *vaapas*{back}
LV1 = *karanaa*{to do}
LV2 = *denaa*{to give}
or
CP = CP+LV
CP = *vaapas karanaa*{to return}
LV = *denaa*{to give}
usane pustak vaapas kar diyaa.
उसने पुस्तक वापस कर दिया
{he book back do gave}

he returned the book.

Here there are two Hindi light verbs used. The verb *kar* (do) is the stem form of the light verb *karanaa* (to do) and the verb *diyaa* (gave) is the past tense form of the light verb *denaa* (to give). The preceding word *vaapas* (back) is an adverb. One way of interpretation is that the CP (a conjunct verb) *vaapas karanaa* (to return) is followed by another LV *denaa* (to give) signifying completion of the task. Another way of looking at it is to consider these as a combination of two CPs, *vaapas karanaa* (to return) and *kar denaa* (to complete the act). The semantic interpretations in the two cases remain the same. It may be noted that the word *vaapas* (return) is also a noun and in such a case the CP is a noun+LV.

From all the above examples, the complexity of the task of mining the CPs is evident. However, it is also observed that in the translated text, the meaning of the light verb does not appear in case of CPs. Our methodology for mining CPs is based on this observation and is outlined in the following section.

3 System Design

As outlined earlier, our method for detecting a CP is based on detecting a mismatch of the Hindi light verb meaning in the aligned English sentence. The steps involved are as follows:

1) Align the sentences of Hindi-English corpus;
2) Create a list of Hindi light verbs and their common English meanings as a simple verb; (Table 1)
3) For each Hindi light verb, generate all the morphological forms (Figure 1);
4) For each English meaning of the light verb as given in table 1, generate all the morphological forms (Figure 2);
5) For each Hindi-English aligned sentence, execute the following steps:
    a) For each light verb of Hindi (table 1), execute the following steps:
        i) Search for a Hindi light verb (LV) and its morphological derivatives (figure 1) in the Hindi sentence and mark its position in the sentence (K);
        ii) If the LV or its morphological derivative is found, then search for the equivalent English meanings for any of the morphological forms (figure 2) in the corresponding aligned English sentence;
        iii) If no match is found, then scan the words in the Hindi sentence to the left of the Kth position (as identified in step (i)); else if a match is found, then exit {i.e. go to step (a)}.
        iv) If the scanned word is a 'stop word' (figure 3), then ignore it and continue scanning;
        v) Stop the scan when it is not a 'stop word' and collect the Hindi word (W);
        vi) If W is an 'exit word' then exit {i.e. go to step (a)}, else the identified CP is W+LV.

Hindi has a large number of light verbs. A list of some of the commonly used light verbs along with their common English meanings as a simple verb is given in table 1. The light verb *kar* (do) is the most frequently used light verb. Using its literal meaning as 'do', as a criterion for testing CP is quite misleading since 'do' in English is used in several other contexts. Such meanings have been shown within parentheses and are not used for matching.

light verb base form	root verb meaning
baithanaa बैठना	sit
bananaa बनना	make/become/build/construct/ manufacture/prepare
banaanaa बनाना	make/build/construct/manufact-ure/ prepare
denaa देना	give
lenaa लेना	take
paanaa पाना	obtain/get
uthanaa उठना	rise/ arise/ get-up
uthaanaa उठाना	raise/lift/ wake-up
laganaa लगना	feel/appear/ look /seem
lagaanaa लगाना	fix/install/ apply
cukanaa चुकना	(finish)
cukaanaa चुकाना	pay
karanaa करना	(do)
honaa होना	happen/become /be
aanaa आना	come
jaanaa जाना	go
khaanaa खाना	eat
rakhanaa रखना	keep / put
maaranaa मारना	kill/beat/hit
daalanaa डालना	put
haankanaa हाँकना	drive

Table 1. Some of the common light verbs in Hindi

For each of the Hindi light verb, all morphological forms are generated. A few illustrations are given in figures 1(a) and 1(b). Similarly, for each of the English meaning of the light verb, all of its morphological derivatives are generated. Figure 2 shows a few illustrations of the same.

There are a number of words that can appear in between the nominal and the light verb in a CP. These words are ignored in search for a CP and are treated as stop words. These are words that denote negation or are emphasizers, intensifiers, interrogative pronoun or a particle. A list of stop words used in the experimentation is given in figure 3.

LV: jaanaa जाना {to go}
Morphological derivatives:
jaa jaae jaao jaae.M jaauu.M jaane jaanaa jaanii jaataa jaatii jaate jaanii.M jaatii.M jaaoge jaaogii gaii jaauu.MgA jaayegaa jaauu.Mgii jaayegii gaye gaii.M gayaa gayii jaaye.Mge jaaye.MgI jaakara

जा (go: stem) जाए (go: imperative)
जाओ (go: imperative) जाएं (go: imperative)
जाऊँ (go: first-person) जाने (go: infinitive, oblique)
जाना (go: infinitive, masculine, singular)
जानी (go: infinitive, feminine, singular)
जाता (go: indefinite, masculine, singular)
जाती (go: indefinite, feminine, singular)
जाते (go: indefinite, masculine, plural/oblique)
जानीं (go: infinitive, feminine, plural)
जातीं (go: indefinite, feminine, plural)
जाओगे (go: future, masculine, singular)
जाओगी (go: future, feminine, singular)
गई (go: past, feminine, singular)
जाऊँगा (go: future, masculine, first-person, singular)
जायेगा (go: future, masculine, third-person, singular)
जाऊँगी (go: future, feminine, first-person, singular)
जायेगी (go: future, feminine, third-person, singular)
गये (go: past, masculine, plural/oblique)
गईं (go: past, feminine, plural)
गया (go: past, masculine, singular)
गयी (go: past, feminine, singular)
जायेंगे (go: future, masculine, plural)
जायेंगी (go: future, feminine, plural)
जाकर (go: completion)
ooooo

Figure 1(a). Morphological derivatives of sample Hindi light verb 'jaanaa' जाना {to go}

LV: lenaa लेना {to take}
Morphological derivatives:
le lii le.M lo letaa letii lete lii.M luu.M legaa legii lene lenaa lenii liyaa le.Mge loge letii.M luu.Mgaa luu.Mgii lekara

ले (take: stem) ली (take: past)
लें (take: imperative) लो (take: imperative)
लेता (take: indefinite, masculine, singular)
लेती (take: indefinite, feminine, singular)
लेते (take: indefinite, masculine, plural/oblique)
लीं(take:past,feminine,plural) लूँ(take: first-person)
लेगा(take: future, masculine, third-person,singular)
लेगी(take: future, feminine, third-person, singular)
लेने (take: infinitive, oblique)
लेना (take: infinitive, masculine, singular)
लेनी (take: infinitive, feminine, singular)
लिया (take: past, masculine, singular)
लेंगे (take: future, masculine, plural)
लोगे (take: future, masculine, singular)
लेतीं (take: indefinite, feminine, plural)
लूँगा (take: future, masculine,first-person,singular)
लूँगी (take: future, feminine, first-person, singular)
लेकर (take: completion)
ooooo

Figure 1(b). Morphological derivatives of sample Hindi light verb 'lenaa' लेना {to take}

English word: sit
Morphological derivations:
`sit sits sat sitting`
English word: give
Morphological derivations:
`give gives gave given giving`
ooooo

Figure 2. Morphological derivatives of sample English meanings

We use a list of words of words that we have named as 'exit words' which cannot form part of a CP in Hindi. We have used Hindi case (*vibhakti*) markers (also called *parsarg*), conjunctions and pronouns as the 'exit words' in our implementation. Figure 4 shows a partial list used. However, this list can be augmented based on analysis of errors in LV identification. It should be noted that we do not perform parts of speech (POS) tagging and so the nature of the word preceding the LV is unknown to the system.

```
नहीं (no/not),
न (no/not /Hindi particle),
भी (also /Hindi particle),
ही(only /Hindi particle),
तो (then /Hindi particle),
क्यों (why),
क्या (what /Hindi particle),
कहाँ (where /Hindi particle),
कब (when),
यहाँ (here),
वहां (there),
जहाँ (where),
पहले (before),
बाद में (after),
शुरू में (beginning),
आरम्भ में (beginning),
अंत में (in the end),
आखिरी में (in the end).
```

Figure 3. Stop words in Hindi used by the system

ने (ergative case marker), को (accusative case marker), का (possessive case marker), के (possessive case marker), की (possessive case marker), से (from/by/with), में (in/into), पर (on/but), और (and/ Hindi particle), तथा (and), या (or), लेकिन (but), परन्तु (but), कि (that/ Hindi particle), मैं (I), तुम (you), आप (you), वह (he/she), मेरा (my), मेरी (my), मेरे (my), तुम्हारा (your), तुम्हारी (your), तुम्हारे (your), उसका (his), उसकी (her), उसके (his/her), अपना (own), अपनी (own), अपने (own), उनके (their), मैंने (I ergative), तुम्हे (to you), आपको (to you), उसको (to him/her), उनको (to them), उन्हें (to them), मुझको (to me), मुझे (to me), जिसका (whose), जिसकी (whose), जिसके (whose), जिनको (to whom), जिनके (to whom)

Figure 4. A few exit words in Hindi used by the system

The inner loop of the procedure identifies multiple CPs that may be present in a sentence. The outer loop is for mining the CPs in the entire corpus. The experimentation and results are discussed in the following section.

4 Experimentation and Results

The CP mining methodology outlined earlier has been implemented and tested over multiple files of EMILLE (McEnery, Baker, Gaizauskas and Cunningham, 2000) English-Hindi parallel corpus. A summary of the results obtained are given in table 2. As can be seen from this table, the precision obtained is 80% to 92% and the recall is between 89% to 100%. The F-measure is 88% to 97%. This is a remarkable and somewhat surprising result from the simple methodology without much of linguistic or statistical analysis. This is much higher than what has been reported on the same corpus by Mukerjee et al, 2006 (83% precision and 46% recall) who use projection of POS and word alignment for CP identification. This is the only other work that uses a parallel corpus and covers all kinds of CPs. The results as reported by Chakrabarti et al. (2008) are only for V-V CPs. Moreover they do not report the recall value.

	File 1	File 2	File 3	File 4	File 5	File 6
No. of Sentences	112	193	102	43	133	107
Total no. of CP(N)	200	298	150	46	188	151
Correctly identified CP (TP)	195	296	149	46	175	135
V-V CP	56	63	9	6	15	20
Incorrectly identified CP (FP)	17	44	7	11	16	20
Unidentified CP (FN)	5	2	1	0	13	16
Accuracy %	97.50	99.33	99.33	100,0	93.08	89.40
Precision % (TP/ (TP+FP))	91.98	87.05	95.51	80.70	91.62	87.09
Recall % (TP / (TP+FN))	97.50	98.33	99.33	100.0	93.08	89.40
F-measure % (2PR / (P+R))	94.6	92.3	97.4	89.3	92.3	88.2

Table 2. Results of the experimentation

Given below are some sample outputs:

(1)
English sentence:
I also enjoy working with the children's parents who often come to me for advice - it's good to know you can help.

Aligned Hindi sentence:
मुझे बच्चों के माता - पिताओं के साथ काम करना भी अच्छा लगता है जो कि अक्सर सलाह लेने आते हैं - यह जानकार खुशी होती है कि आप किसी की मदद कर सकते हैं ।

The CPs identified in the sentence:
i. काम करना (to work), ii. अच्छा लगना (to feel good: enjoy), iii. सलाह लेना (to seek advice), iv. खुशी होना (to feel happy: good), v. मदद करना (to help)

Here the system identified 5 different CPs all of which are correct and no CP in the sentence has gone undetected. The POS projection and word alignment method (Mukerjee et al., 2006) would fail to identify CPs सलाह लेना (to seek advice), and खुशी होना (to feel happy).

(2)
English sentence:
Thousands of children are already benefiting from the input of people like you - people who care about children and their future, who have the commitment, energy and enthusiasm to be positive role models, and who value the opportunity for a worthwhile career.

Aligned Hindi sentence:
आप जैसे लोग जो कि बच्चों और उनके भविष्य के बारे में सोचते हैं - इस समय भी हज़ारों बच्चों को लाभ पहुँचा रहे हैं । अच्छे आदर्श बनने के लिए ऐसे लोगों में प्रतिबद्धता , उत्सराह और लगन है और वे एक समर्थन - योग्य व्यवसाय की कद्र करते हैं ।

The CPs identified in the sentence:
i. आदर्श बनना (to be role model), ii. कद्र करना (to respect)

Here also the two CPs identified are correct.

It is obvious that this empirical method of mining CPs will fail whenever the Hindi light verb maps on to its core meaning in English. It may also produce garbage as POS of the preceding word is not being checked. However, the mining success rate obtained speaks of these being in small numbers in practice. Use of the 'stop words' in allowing the intervening words within the CPs helps a lot in improving the performance. Similarly, use of the 'exit words' avoid a lot of incorrect identification.

5 Conclusions

The simple empirical method for mining CPs outlined in this work, yields an average 89% of precision and 90% recall which is better than the results reported so far in the literature. The major drawback is that we have to generate a list of all possible light verbs. This list appears to be very large for Hindi. Since no POS tagging or statistical analysis is performed, the identified CPs are merely a list of mined CPs in Hindi with no linguistic categorization or analysis. However, this list of mined CPs is valuable to the lexicographers and other language technology developers. This list can also be used for word alignment tools where the identified components of CPs are grouped together before the word alignment process. This will increase both the alignment accuracy and the speed.

The methodology presented in this work is equally applicable to all other languages within the Indo-Aryan family.

References

Anthony McEnery, Paul Baker, Rob Gaizauskas, Hamish Cunningham. 2000. EMILLE: Building a Corpus of South Asian Languages, *Vivek, A Quarterly in Artiificial Intelligence,* 13(3):23–32.

Amitabh Mukerjee, Ankit Soni, and Achala M. Raina, 2006. Detecting Complex Predicates in Hindi using POS Projection across Parallel Corpora, *Proceedings of the Workshop on Multiword Expressions: Identifying and Exploiting Underlying Properties*, Sydney, 11–18,

Alex Alsina. 1996. *Complex Predicates:Structure and Theory*. CSLI Publications,Stanford, CA.

Anvita Abbi. 1992. The explicator compound verb:some definitional issues and criteria for identification. *Indian Linguistics*, 53, 27-46.

Debasri Chakrabarti, Vaijayanthi Sarma and Pushpak Bhattacharyya. 2007. Complex Predicates in Indian Language Wordnets, *Lexical Resources and Evaluation Journal*, 40 (3-4).

Debasri Chakrabarti, Hemang Mandalia, Ritwik Priya, Vaijayanthi Sarma and Pushpak Bhattacharyya. 2008. Hindi Compound Verbs and their Automatic Extraction, *Computational Linguistics (COLING08),* Manchester, UK.

Manindra K. Verma (ed.) 1993. *Complex Predicates in South Asian Languages.* Manohar Publishers and Distributors, New Delhi

Miriam Butt. 1995. *The Structure of Complex Predicates in Urdu.* CSLI Publications.

Mirium Butt and Gillian Ramchand. 2001. *Complex Aspectual Structure in Hindi/Urdu.* In Maria Liakata, Britta Jensen and Didier Maillat (Editors), Oxford University Working Papers in Linguistics, Philology & Phonetics, Vol. 6.

Miriam Butt, Tracy Holloway King, and John T. Maxwell III. 2003. Complex Predicates via Restriction, *Proceedings of the LFG03 Conference.*

Miriam Butt and Wilhelm Geuder. 2001. *On the (semi)lexical status of light verbs.* In Norbert Corver and Henk van Riemsdijk, (Editors), Semi-lexical Categories: On the content of function words and the function of content words, Mouton de Gruyter, Berlin, 323–370.

Mona Singh. 1994. *Perfectivity, Definiteness, and Specificity: A Classification of Verbal Predicates Hindi.* Doctoral dissertation, University of Texas, Austin.

Peter Edwin Hook. 1974. *The Compound Verb in Hindi.* Center for South and Southeast Asian Studies: The University of Michigan.

Tara Mohanan. 1994. *Argument Structure in Hindi.* CSLI Publications, Stanford, California

Venkatapathy Sriram and Aravind K. Joshi, 2005. Relative compositionality of multi-word expressions: a study of verb-noun (V-N) collocations, *In Proceedings of International Joint Conference on Natural Language Processing - 2005, Jeju Island, Korea,* 553-564.

Improving Statistical Machine Translation Using Domain Bilingual Multiword Expressions

Zhixiang Ren[1] **Yajuan Lü**[1] **Jie Cao**[1] **Qun Liu**[1] **Yun Huang**[2]

[1]Key Lab. of Intelligent Info. Processing
Institute of Computing Technology
Chinese Academy of Sciences
P.O. Box 2704, Beijing 100190, China
{renzhixiang,lvyajuan
caojie,liuqun}@ict.ac.cn

[2]Department of Computer Science
School of Computing
National University of Singapore
Computing 1, Law Link, Singapore 117590
huangyun@comp.nus.edu.sg

Abstract

Multiword expressions (MWEs) have been proved useful for many natural language processing tasks. However, how to use them to improve performance of statistical machine translation (SMT) is not well studied. This paper presents a simple yet effective strategy to extract domain bilingual multiword expressions. In addition, we implement three methods to integrate bilingual MWEs to Moses, the state-of-the-art phrase-based machine translation system. Experiments show that bilingual MWEs could improve translation performance significantly.

1 Introduction

Phrase-based machine translation model has been proved a great improvement over the initial word-based approaches (Brown et al., 1993). Recent syntax-based models perform even better than phrase-based models. However, when syntax-based models are applied to new domain with few syntax-annotated corpus, the translation performance would decrease. To utilize the robustness of phrases and make up the lack of syntax or semantic information in phrase-based model for domain translation, we study domain bilingual multiword expressions and integrate them to the existing phrase-based model.

A *multiword expression (MWE)* can be considered as word sequence with relatively fixed structure representing special meanings. There is no uniform definition of MWE, and many researchers give different properties of MWE. Sag et al. (2002) roughly defined MWE as "idiosyncratic interpretations that cross word boundaries (or spaces)". Cruys and Moirón (2007) focused on the non-compositional property of MWE, i.e. the property that whole expression cannot be derived from their component words. Stanford university launched a MWE project[1], in which different qualities of MWE were presented. For *bilingual multiword expression (BiMWE)*, we define a bilingual phrase as a bilingual MWE if (1) the source phrase is a MWE in source language; (2) the source phrase and the target phrase must be translated to each other exactly, i.e. there is no additional (boundary) word in target phrase which cannot find the corresponding word in source phrase, and vice versa. In recent years, many useful methods have been proposed to extract MWEs or BiMWEs automatically (Piao et al., 2005; Bannard, 2007; Fazly and Stevenson, 2006). Since MWE usually constrains possible senses of a polysemous word in context, they can be used in many NLP applications such as information retrieval, question answering, word sense disambiguation and so on.

For machine translation, Piao et al. (2005) have noted that the issue of MWE identification and accurate interpretation from source to target language remained an unsolved problem for existing MT systems. This problem is more severe when MT systems are used to translate domain-specific texts, since they may include technical terminology as well as more general fixed expressions and idioms. Although some MT systems may employ a machine-readable bilingual dictionary of MWE, it is time-consuming and inefficient to obtain this resource manually. Therefore, some researchers have tried to use automatically extracted bilingual MWEs in SMT. Tanaka and Baldwin (2003) described an approach of noun-noun compound machine translation, but no significant comparison was presented. Lambert and Banchs (2005) presented a method in which bilingual MWEs were used to modify the word alignment so as to improve the SMT quality. In their work, a bilingual MWE in training corpus was grouped as

[1]http://mwe.stanford.edu/

Proceedings of the 2009 Workshop on Multiword Expressions, ACL-IJCNLP 2009, pages 47–54,
Suntec, Singapore, 6 August 2009. ©2009 ACL and AFNLP

one unique token before training alignment models. They reported that both alignment quality and translation accuracy were improved on a small corpus. However, in their further study, they reported even lower BLEU scores after grouping MWEs according to part-of-speech on a large corpus (Lambert and Banchs, 2006). Nonetheless, since MWE represents liguistic knowledge, the role and usefulness of MWE in full-scale SMT is intuitively positive. The difficulty lies in how to integrate bilingual MWEs into existing SMT system to improve SMT performance, especially when translating domain texts.

In this paper, we implement three methods that integrate domain bilingual MWEs into a phrase-based SMT system, and show that these approaches improve translation quality significantly. The main difference between our methods and Lambert and Banchs' work is that we directly aim at improving the SMT performance rather than improving the word alignment quality. In detail, differences are listed as follows:

- Instead of using the bilingual n-gram translation model, we choose the phrase-based SMT system, Moses[2], which achieves significantly better translation performance than many other SMT systems and is a state-of-the-art SMT system.

- Instead of improving translation indirectly by improving the word alignment quality, we directly target at the quality of translation. Some researchers have argued that large gains of alignment performance under many metrics only led to small gains in translation performance (Ayan and Dorr, 2006; Fraser and Marcu, 2007).

Besides the above differences, there are some advantages of our approaches:

- In our method, automatically extracted MWEs are used as additional resources rather than as phrase-table filter. Since bilingual MWEs are extracted according to noisy automatic word alignment, errors in word alignment would further propagate to the SMT and hurt SMT performance.

- We conduct experiments on domain-specific corpus. For one thing, domain-specific corpus potentially includes a large number of technical terminologies as well as more general fixed expressions and idioms, i.e. domain-specific corpus has high MWE coverage. For another, after the investigation, current SMT system could not effectively deal with these domain-specific MWEs especially for Chinese, since these MWEs are more flexible and concise. Take the Chinese term "软坚散结" for example. The meaning of this term is "soften hard mass and dispel pathogenic accumulation". Every word of this term represents a special meaning and cannot be understood literally or without this context. These terms are difficult to be translated even for humans, let alone machine translation. So, treating these terms as MWEs and applying them in SMT system have practical significance.

- In our approach, no additional corpus is introduced. We attempt to extract useful MWEs from the training corpus and adopt suitable methods to apply them. Thus, it benefits for the full exploitation of available resources without increasing great time and space complexities of SMT system.

The remainder of the paper is organized as follows. Section 2 describes the bilingual MWE extraction technique. Section 3 proposes three methods to apply bilingual MWEs in SMT system. Section 4 presents the experimental results. Section 5 draws conclusions and describes the future work. Since this paper mainly focuses on the application of BiMWE in SMT, we only give a brief introduction on monolingual and bilingual MWE extraction.

2 Bilingual Multiword Expression Extraction

In this section we describe our approach of bilingual MWE extraction. In the first step, we obtain monolingual MWEs from the Chinese part of parallel corpus. After that, we look for the translation of the extracted MWEs from parallel corpus.

2.1 Automatic Extraction of MWEs

In the past two decades, many different approaches on automatic MWE identification were reported. In general, those approaches can be classified into three main trends: (1) statistical approaches (Pantel and Lin, 2001; Piao et

[2]http://www.statmt.org/moses/

al., 2005), (2) syntactic approaches (Fazly and Stevenson, 2006; Bannard, 2007), and (3) semantic approaches (Baldwin et al., 2003; Cruys and Moirón, 2007). Syntax-based and semantic-based methods achieve high precision, but syntax or semantic analysis has to be introduced as preparing step, so it is difficult to apply them to domains with few syntactical or semantic annotation. Statistical approaches only consider frequency information, so they can be used to obtain MWEs from bilingual corpora without deeper syntactic or semantic analysis. Most statistical measures only take two words into account, so it not easy to extract MWEs containing three or more than three words.

Log Likelihood Ratio (LLR) has been proved a good statistical measurement of the association of two random variables (Chang et al., 2002). We adopt the idea of statistical approaches, and propose a new algorithm named LLR-based Hierarchical Reducing Algorithm (HRA for short) to extract MWEs with arbitrary lengths. To illustrate our algorithm, firstly we define some useful items. In the following definitions, we assume the given sentence is "*A B C D E*".

Definition 1 *Unit:* A unit is any sub-string of the given sentence. For example, "*A B*", "*C*", "*C D E*" are all units, but "*A B D*" is not a unit.

Definition 2 *List:* A list is an ordered sequence of units which exactly cover the given sentence. For example, {"*A*","*B C D*","*E*"} forms a list.

Definition 3 *Score:* The score function only defines on two adjacent units and return the LLR between the last word of first unit and the first word of the second unit[3]. For example, the score of adjacent unit "*B C*" and "*D E*" is defined as LLR("*C*","*D*").

Definition 4 *Select:* The selecting operator is to find the two adjacent units with maximum score in a list.

Definition 5 *Reduce:* The reducing operator is to remove two specific adjacent units, concatenate them, and put back the result unit to the removed position. For example, if we want to reduce unit "*B C*" and unit "*D*" in list {"*A*","*B C*","*D*","*E*"}, we will get the list {"*A*","*B C D*","*E*"}.

Initially, every word in the sentence is considered as one unit and all these units form a initial list L. If the sentence is of length N, then the list contains N units, of course. The final set of MWEs, S, is initialized to empty set. After initialization, the algorithm will enter an iterating loop with two steps: (1) select the two adjacent units with maximum score in L, naming U_1 and U_2; and (2) reduce U_1 and U_2 in L, and insert the reducing result into the final set S. Our algorithm terminates on two conditions: (1) if the maximum score after selection is less than a given threshold; or (2) if L contains only one unit.

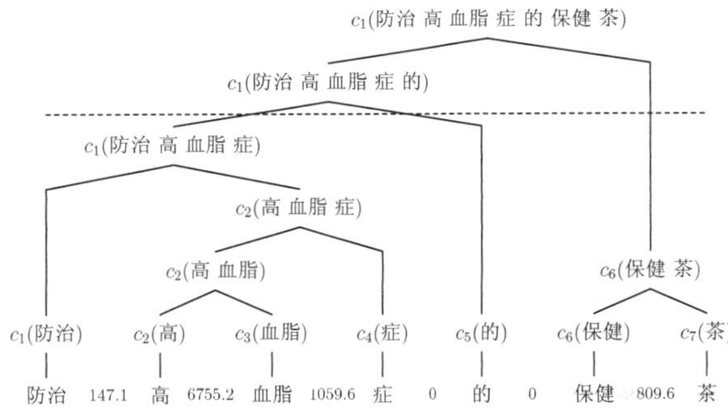

Figure 1: Example of Hierarchical Reducing Algorithm

Let us make the algorithm clearer with an example. Assume the threshold of score is 20, the given sentence is "*防治 高 血脂 症 的 保健 茶*"[4]. Figure 1 shows the hierarchical structure of given sentence (based on LLR of adjacent words). In this example, four MWEs ("*高 血脂*", "*高 血脂 症*", "*保健 茶*", "*防治 高 血脂 症*") are extracted in the order, and sub-strings over dotted line in figure 1 are not extracted.

From the above example, we can see that the extracted MWEs correspond to human intuition. In general, the basic idea of HRA is to reflect the hierarchical structure pattern of natural language. Furthermore, in the HRA, MWEs are measured with the minimum LLR of adjacent words in them, which gives lexical confidence of extracted MWEs. Finally, suppose given sentence has length N, HRA would definitely terminate within $N - 1$ iterations, which is very efficient.

However, HRA has a problem that it would extract substrings before extracting the whole string, even if the substrings only appear in the particular whole string, which we consider useless. To solve this problem, we use contextual features,

[3] we use a stoplist to eliminate the units containing function words by setting their score to 0

[4] The whole sentence means "healthy tea for preventing hyperlipidemia", and we give the meaning for each Chinese word: 防治(preventing), 高(hyper-), 血脂(-lipid-), 症(-emia), 的(for), 保健(healthy), 茶(tea).

contextual entropy (Luo and Sun, 2003) and C-value (Frantzi and Ananiadou, 1996), to filter out those substrings which exist only in few MWEs.

2.2 Automatic Extraction of MWE's Translation

In subsection 2.1, we described the algorithm to obtain MWEs, and we would like to introduce the procedure to find their translations from parallel corpus in this subsection.

For mining the English translations of Chinese MWEs, we first obtain the candidate translations of a given MWE from the parallel corpus. Steps are listed as follows:

1. Run GIZA++[5] to align words in the training parallel corpus.

2. For a given MWE, find the bilingual sentence pairs where the source language sentences include the MWE.

3. Extract the candidate translations of the MWE from the above sentence pairs according to the algorithm described by Och (2002).

After the above procedure, we have already extracted all possible candidate translations of a given MWE. The next step is to distinguish right candidates from wrong candidates. We construct perceptron-based classification model (Collins, 2002) to solve the problem. We design two groups of features: translation features, which describe the mutual translating chance between source phrase and target phrase, and the language features, which refer to how well a candidate is a reasonable translation. The translation features include: (1) the logarithm of source-target translation probability; (2) the logarithm of target-source translation probability; (3) the logarithm of source-target lexical weighting; (4) the logarithm of target-source lexical weighting; and (5) the logarithm of the phrase pair's LLR (Dunning, 1993). The first four features are exactly the same as the four translation probabilities used in traditional phrase-based system (Koehn et al., 2003). The language features include: (1) the left entropy of the target phrase (Luo and Sun, 2003); (2) the right entropy of the target phrase; (3) the first word of the target phrase; (4) the last word of the target phrase; and (5) all words in the target phrase.

[5]http://www.fjoch.com/GIZA++.html

We select and annotate 33000 phrase pairs randomly, of which 30000 pairs are used as training set and 3000 pairs are used as test set. We use the perceptron training algorithm to train the model. As the experiments reveal, the classification precision of this model is 91.67%.

3 Application of Bilingual MWEs

Intuitively, bilingual MWE is useful to improve the performance of SMT. However, as we described in section 1, it still needs further research on how to integrate bilingual MWEs into SMT system. In this section, we propose three methods to utilize bilingual MWEs, and we will compare their performance in section 4.

3.1 Model Retraining with Bilingual MWEs

Bilingual phrase table is very important for phrase-based MT system. However, due to the errors in automatic word alignment and unaligned word extension in phrase extraction (Och, 2002), many meaningless phrases would be extracted, which results in inaccuracy of phrase probability estimation. To alleviate this problem, we take the automatically extracted bilingual MWEs as parallel sentence pairs, add them into the training corpus, and retrain the model using GIZA++. By increasing the occurrences of bilingual MWEs, which are good phrases, we expect that the alignment would be modified and the probability estimation would be more reasonable. Wu et al. (2008) also used this method to perform domain adaption for SMT. Different from their approach, in which bilingual MWEs are extracted from additional corpus, we extract bilingual MWEs from the original training set. The fact that additional resources can improve the domain-specific SMT performance was proved by many researchers (Wu et al., 2008; Eck et al., 2004). However, our method shows that making better use of the resources in hand could also enhance the quality of SMT system. We use "Baseline+BiMWE" to represent this method.

3.2 New Feature for Bilingual MWEs

Lopez and Resnik (2006) once pointed out that better feature mining can lead to substantial gain in translation quality. Inspired by this idea, we append one feature into bilingual phrase table to indicate that whether a bilingual phrase contains bilingual MWEs. In other words, if the source language phrase contains a MWE (as substring) and the target language phrase contains the translation of the MWE (as substring), the feature value is 1, otherwise the feature value is set to 0. Due to the high reliability of bilingual MWEs, we expect that this feature could help SMT system to select better and reasonable phrase pairs during translation. We use "Baseline+Feat" to represent this method.

3.3 Additional Phrase Table of bilingual MWEs

Wu et al. (2008) proposed a method to construct a phrase table by a manually-made translation dictionary. Instead of manually constructing translation dictionary, we construct an additional phrase table containing automatically extracted bilingual MWEs. As to probability assignment, we just assign 1 to the four translation probabilities for simplicity. Since Moses supports multiple bilingual phrase tables, we combine the original phrase table and new constructed bilingual MWE table. For each phrase in input sentence during translation, the decoder would search all candidate translation phrases in both phrase tables. We use "Baseline+NewBP" to represent this method.

4 Experiments

4.1 Data

We run experiments on two domain-specific patent corpora: one is for traditional medicine domain, and the other is for chemical industry domain. Our translation tasks are Chinese-to-English.

In the traditional medicine domain, table 1 shows the data statistics. For language model, we use SRI Language Modeling Toolkit[6] to train a trigram model with modified Kneser-Ney smoothing (Chen and Goodman, 1998) on the target side of training corpus. Using our bilingual MWE extracting algorithm, 80287 bilingual MWEs are extracted from the training set.

	Chinese	English
Training Sentences	120,355	
Words	4,688,873	4,737,843
Dev Sentences	1,000	
Words	31,722	32,390
Test Sentences	1,000	
Words	41,643	40,551

Table 1: Traditional medicine corpus

[6]http://www.speech.sri.com/projects/srilm/

In the chemical industry domain, table 2 gives the detail information of the data. In this experiment, 59466 bilingual MWEs are extracted.

	Chinese	English
Training Sentences	120,856	
Words	4,532,503	4,311,682
Dev Sentences	1,099	
Words	42,122	40,521
Test Sentences	1,099	
Words	41,069	39,210

Table 2: Chemical industry corpus

We test translation quality on test set and use the open source tool mteval-vllb.pl[7] to calculate case-sensitive BLEU 4 score (Papineni et al., 2002) as our evaluation criteria. For this evaluation, there is only one reference per test sentence. We also perform statistical significant test between two translation results (Collins et al., 2005). The mean of all scores and relative standard deviation are calculated with a 99% confidence interval of the mean.

4.2 MT Systems

We use the state-of-the-art phrase-based SMT system, Moses, as our baseline system. The features used in baseline system include: (1) four translation probability features; (2) one language model feature; (3) distance-based and lexicalized distortion model feature; (4) word penalty; (5) phrase penalty. For "Baseline+BiMWE" method, bilingual MWEs are added into training corpus, as a result, new alignment and new phrase table are obtained. For "Baseline+Feat" method, one additional 0/1 feature are introduced to each entry in phrase table. For "Baseline+NewBP", additional phrase table constructed by bilingual MWEs is used.

Features are combined in the log-linear model. To obtain the best translation $\hat{e}$ of the source sentence f, log-linear model uses following equation:

$$\begin{aligned} \hat{e} &= \arg\max_{e} p(e|f) \\ &= \arg\max_{e} \sum_{m=1}^{M} \lambda_m h_m(e,f) \end{aligned} \quad (1)$$

in which h_m and λ_m denote the mth feature and weight. The weights are automatically turned by minimum error rate training (Och, 2002) on development set.

[7]http://www.nist.gov/speech/tests/mt/resources/scoring.htm

4.3 Results

Methods	BLEU
Baseline	0.2658
Baseline+BiMWE	0.2661
Baseline+Feat	0.2675
Baseline+NewBP	0.2719

Table 3: Translation results of using bilingual MWEs in traditional medicine domain

Table 3 gives our experiment results. From this table, we can see that, bilingual MWEs improve translation quality in all cases. The Baseline+NewBP method achieves the most improvement of 0.61% BLEU score compared with the baseline system. The Baseline+Feat method comes next with 0.17% BLEU score improvement. And the Baseline+BiMWE achieves slightly higher translation quality than the baseline system.

To our disappointment, however, none of these improvements are statistical significant. We manually examine the extracted bilingual MWEs which are labeled positive by perceptron algorithm and find that although the classification precision is high (91.67%), the proportion of positive example is relatively lower (76.69%). The low positive proportion means that many negative instances have been wrongly classified to positive, which introduce noises. To remove noisy bilingual MWEs, we use the length ratio x of the source phrase over the target phrase to rank the bilingual MWEs labeled positive. Assume x follows Gaussian distributions, then the ranking score of phrase pair (s, t) is defined as the following formula:

$$Score(s,t) = \log(LLR(s,t)) \times \frac{1}{\sqrt{2\pi}\sigma} \times e^{-\frac{(x-\mu)^2}{2\sigma^2}} \quad (2)$$

Here the mean μ and variance σ^2 are estimated from the training set. After ranking by score, we select the top 50000, 60000 and 70000 bilingual MWEs to perform the three methods mentioned in section 3. The results are showed in table 4.

From this table, we can conclude that: (1) All the three methods on all settings improve BLEU score; (2) Except the Baseline+BiMWE method, the other two methods obtain significant improvement of BLEU score (0.2728, 0.2734, 0.2724) over baseline system (0.2658); (3) When the scale of bilingual MWEs is relatively small (50000, 60000), the Baseline+Feat method performs better

Methods	50000	60000	70000
Baseline		0.2658	
Baseline+BiMWE	0.2671	0.2686	0.2715
Baseline+Feat	**0.2728**	**0.2734**	0.2712
Baseline+NewBP	0.2662	0.2706	**0.2724**

Table 4: Translation results of using bilingual MWEs in traditional medicine domain

than others; (4) As the number of bilingual MWEs increasing, the Baseline+NewBP method outperforms the Baseline+Feat method; (5) Comparing table 4 and 3, we can see it is not true that the more bilingual MWEs, the better performance of phrase-based SMT. This conclusion is the same as (Lambert and Banchs, 2005).

To verify the assumption that bilingual MWEs do indeed improve the SMT performance not only on particular domain, we also perform some experiments on chemical industry domain. Table 5 shows the results. From this table, we can see that these three methods can improve the translation performance on chemical industry domain as well as on the traditional medicine domain.

Methods	BLEU
Baseline	0.1882
Baseline+BiMWE	0.1928
Baseline+Feat	0.1917
Baseline+Newbp	0.1914

Table 5: Translation results of using bilingual MWEs in chemical industry domain

4.4 Discussion

In order to know in what respects our methods improve performance of translation, we manually analyze some test sentences and gives some examples in this subsection.

(1) For the first example in table 6, "*通脉*" is aligned to other words and not correctly translated in baseline system, while it is aligned to correct target phrase "*dredging meridians*" in Baseline+BiMWE, since the bilingual MWE ("*通脉*", "*dredging meridians*") has been added into training corpus and then aligned by GIZA++.

(2) For the second example in table 6, "*药茶*" has two candidate translation in phrase table: "*tea*" and "*medicated tea*". The baseline system chooses the "*tea*" as the translation of "*药茶*", while the Baseline+Feat system chooses the "*med-*

Src	该食品具有补血、逐寒、通脉、生津、利水、安神等滋补功效,可达到健身营养的目的。
Ref	the obtained product is effective in tonifying blood , expelling cold , **dredging meridians , promoting production of body fluid , promoting urination** , and tranquilizing mind ; and can be used for supplementing nutrition and protecting health .
Baseline	the food has effects in tonifying blood , dispelling cold , **promoting salivation and water** , and tranquilizing , and tonic effects , and making nutritious health .
+Bimwe	the food has effects in tonifying blood , dispelling cold , **dredging meridians , promoting salivation , promoting urination** , and tranquilizing tonic , nutritious pulverizing .
Src	还可制成片剂、丸剂、散剂、药茶、注射剂。
Ref	the product can also be made into tablet , pill , powder , **medicated tea** , or injection .
Baseline	may also be made into tablet , pill , powder , **tea** , or injection .
+Feat	may also be made into tablet , pill , powder , **medicated tea** , or injection .

Table 6: Translation example

icated tea" because the additional feature gives high probability of the correct translation "*medicated tea*".

5 Conclusion and Future Works

This paper presents the LLR-based hierarchical reducing algorithm to automatically extract bilingual MWEs and investigates the performance of three different application strategies in applying bilingual MWEs for SMT system. The translation results show that using an additional feature to represent whether a bilingual phrase contains bilingual MWEs performs the best in most cases. The other two strategies can also improve the quality of SMT system, although not as much as the first one. These results are encouraging and motivated to do further research in this area.

The strategies of bilingual MWE application is roughly simply and coarse in this paper. Complicated approaches should be taken into account during applying bilingual MWEs. For example, we may consider other features of the bilingual MWEs and examine their effect on the SMT performance. Besides application in phrase-based SMT system, bilingual MWEs may also be integrated into other MT models such as hierarchical phrase-based models or syntax-based translation models. We will do further studies on improving statistical machine translation using domain bilingual MWEs.

Acknowledgments

This work is supported by National Natural Science Foundation of China, Contracts 60603095 and 60873167. We would like to thank the anonymous reviewers for their insightful comments on an earlier draft of this paper.

References

Necip Fazil Ayan and Bonnie J. Dorr. 2006. Going beyond aer: an extensive analysis of word alignments and their impact on mt. In *Proceedings of the 44th Annual Meeting of the Association for Computational Linguistics*, pages 9–16.

Timothy Baldwin, Colin Bannard, Takaaki Tanaka, and Dominic Widdows. 2003. An empirical model of multiword expression decomposability. In *Proceedings of the ACL-2003 Workshop on Multiword Expressions: Analysis, Acquisiton and Treatment*, pages 89–96.

Colin Bannard. 2007. A measure of syntactic flexibility for automatically identifying multiword expressions in corpora. In *Proceedings of the ACL Workshop on A Broader Perspective on Multiword Expressions*, pages 1–8.

Peter F. Brown, Stephen Della Pietra, Vincent J. Della Pietra, and Robert L. Mercer. 1993. The mathematics of statistical machine translation: Parameter estimation. *Computational Linguistics*, 19(2):263–311.

Baobao Chang, Pernilla Danielsson, and Wolfgang Teubert. 2002. Extraction of translation unit from chinese-english parallel corpora. In *Proceedings of the first SIGHAN workshop on Chinese language processing*, pages 1–5.

Stanley F. Chen and Joshua Goodman. 1998. Am empirical study of smoothing techniques for language modeling. Technical report.

Michael Collins, Philipp Koehn, and Ivona Kučerová. 2005. Clause restructuring for statistical machine translation. In *Proceedings of the 43rd Annual*

Meeting on Association for Computational Linguistics, pages 531–540.

Michael Collins. 2002. Discriminative training methods for hidden markov models: Theory and experiments with perceptron algorithms. In *Proceedings of the Empirical Methods in Natural Language Processing Conference*, pages 1–8.

Tim Van de Cruys and Begoña Villada Moirón. 2007. Semantics-based multiword expression extraction. In *Proceedings of the Workshop on A Broader Perspective on Multiword Expressions*, pages 25–32.

Ted Dunning. 1993. Accurate methods for the statistics of surprise and coincidence. *Computational Linguistics*, 19(1):61–74.

Matthias Eck, Stephan Vogel, and Alex Waibel. 2004. Improving statistical machine translation in the medical domain using the unified medical language system. In *Proceedings of the 20th international conference on Computational Linguistics table of contents*, pages 792–798.

Afsaneh Fazly and Suzanne Stevenson. 2006. Automatically constructing a lexicon of verb phrase idiomatic combinations. In *Proceedings of the EACL*, pages 337–344.

Katerina T. Frantzi and Sophia Ananiadou. 1996. Extracting nested collocations. In *Proceedings of the 16th conference on Computational linguistics*, pages 41–46.

Alexander Fraser and Daniel Marcu. 2007. Measuring word alignment quality for statistical machine translation. *Computational Linguistics*, 33(3):293–303.

Philipp Koehn, Franz Josef Och, and Daniel Marcu. 2003. Statistical phrase-based translation. In *Proceedings of the 2003 Conference of the North American Chapter of the Association for Computational Linguistics on Human Language Technology*, pages 48–54.

Patrik Lambert and Rafael Banchs. 2005. Data inferred multi-word expressions for statistical machine translation. In *Proceedings of Machine Translation Summit X*, pages 396–403.

Patrik Lambert and Rafael Banchs. 2006. Grouping multi-word expressions according to part-of-speech in statistical machine translation. In *Proceedings of the Workshop on Multi-word-expressions in a multilingual context*, pages 9–16.

Adam Lopez and Philip Resnik. 2006. Word-based alignment, phrase-based translation: What's the link? In *proceedings of the 7th conference of the association for machine translation in the Americas: visions for the future of machine translation*, pages 90–99.

Shengfen Luo and Maosong Sun. 2003. Two-character chinese word extraction based on hybrid of internal and contextual measures. In *Proceedings of the second SIGHAN workshop on Chinese language processing*, pages 24–30.

Franz Josef Och. 2002. *Statistical Machine Translation: From Single-Word Models to Alignment Templates*. Ph.d. thesis, Computer Science Department, RWTH Aachen, Germany.

Patrick Pantel and Dekang Lin. 2001. A statistical corpus based term extractor. In *AI '01: Proceedings of the 14th Biennial Conference of the Canadian Society on Computational Studies of Intelligence*, pages 36–46.

Kishore Papineni, Salim Roukos, Todd Ward, and Weijing Zhu. 2002. Bleu: a method for automatic evaluation of machine translation. In *Proceedings of the 40th Annual Conference of the Association for Computational Linguistics*, pages 311–318.

Scott Songlin Piao, Paul Rayson, Dawn Archer, and Tony McEnery. 2005. Comparing and combining a semantic tagger and a statistical tool for mwe extraction. *Computer Speech and Language*, 19(4):378–397.

Ivan A. Sag, Timothy Baldwin, Francis Bond, Ann Copestake, and Dan Flickinger. 2002. Multiword expressions: A pain in the neck for nlp. In *Proceedings of the 3th International Conference on Intelligent Text Processing and Computational Linguistics(CICLing-2002)*, pages 1–15.

Takaaki Tanaka and Timothy Baldwin. 2003. Noun-noun compound machine translation: A feasibility study on shallow processing. In *Proceedings of the ACL-2003 Workshop on Multiword Expressions: Analysis, Acquisition and Treatment*, pages 17–24.

Hua Wu, Haifeng Wang, and Chengqing Zong. 2008. Domain adaptation for statistical machine translation with domain dictionary and monolingual corpora. In *Proceedings of Conference on Computational Linguistics (COLING)*, pages 993–1000.

Bottom-up Named Entity Recognition using a Two-stage Machine Learning Method

Hirotaka Funayama Tomohide Shibata Sadao Kurohashi
Kyoto University, Yoshida-honmachi,
Sakyo-ku, Kyoto, 606-8501, Japan
{funayama, shibata, kuro}@nlp.kuee.kyoto-u.ac.jp

Abstract

This paper proposes Japanese bottom-up named entity recognition using a two-stage machine learning method. Most work has formalized Named Entity Recognition as a sequential labeling problem, in which only local information is utilized for the label estimation, and thus a long named entity consisting of several morphemes tends to be wrongly recognized. Our proposed method regards a compound noun (*chunk*) as a labeling unit, and first estimates the labels of all the chunks in a phrasal unit (*bunsetsu*) using a machine learning method. Then, the best label assignment in the *bunsetsu* is determined from bottom up as the CKY parsing algorithm using a machine learning method. We conducted an experimental on CRL NE data, and achieved an F measure of 89.79, which is higher than previous work.

1 Introduction

Named Entity Recognition (NER) is a task of recognizing named entities such as person names, organization names, and location. It is used for several NLP applications such as Information Extraction (IE) and Question Answering (QA). Most work uses machine learning methods such as Support Vector Machines (SVMs) (Vapnik, 1995) and Conditional Random Field (CRF) (Lafferty et al., 2001) using a hand-annotated corpus (Krishnan and D.Manning, 2006; Kazama and Torisawa, 2008; Sasano and Kurohashi, 2008; Fukushima et al., 2008; Nakano and Hirai, 2004; Masayuki and Matsumoto, 2003).

In general, NER is formalized as a sequential labeling problem. For example, regarding a morpheme as a basic unit, it is first labeled as S-PERSON, B-PERSON, I-PERSON, E-PERSON, S-ORGANIZATION, etc. Then, considering the labeling results of morphemes, the best NE label sequence is recognized.

When the label of each morpheme is estimated, only local information around the morpheme (e.g., the morpheme, the two preceding morphemes, and the two following morphemes) is utilized. Therefore, a long named entity consisting of several morphemes tends to be wrongly recognized. Let us consider the example sentences shown in Figure 1.

In sentence (1), the label of "*Kazama*" can be recognized to be S-PERSON (PERSON consisting of one morpheme) by utilizing the surrounding information such as the suffix "*san*" (Mr.) and the verb "*kikoku shita*" (return home).

On the other hand, in sentence (2), when the label of "*shinyou*" (credit) is recognized to be B-ORGANIZATION (the beginning of ORGANIZATION), only information from "*hatsudou*" (invoke) to "*kyusai*" (relief) can be utilized, and thus the information of the morpheme "*ginkou*" (bank) that is apart from "*shinyou*" by three morphemes cannot be utilized. To cope with this problem, Nakano et al. (Nakano and Hirai, 2004) and Sasano et al. (Sasano and Kurohashi, 2008) utilized information of the head of *bunsetsu*[1]. In their methods, when the label of "*shinyou*" is recognized, the information of the morpheme "*ginkou*" can be utilized.

However, these methods do not work when the morpheme that we want to refer to is not a head of *bunsetsu* as in sentence (3). In this example, when "*gaikoku*" (foreign) is recognized to be B-ARTIFACT (the beginning of ARTIFACT), we want to refer to "*hou*" (law), not "*ihan*" (violation), which is the head of the *bunsetsu*.

This paper proposes Japanese bottom-up named

[1] Bunsetsu is the smallest coherent phrasal unit in Japanese. It consists of one or more content words followed by zero or more function words.

Proceedings of the 2009 Workshop on Multiword Expressions, ACL-IJCNLP 2009, pages 55–62,
Suntec, Singapore, 6 August 2009.

(1) *kikoku-shita Kazama-san-wa ...*
return home Mr.Kazama TOP
'Mr. Kazama who returned home'

(2) *hatsudou-shita shinyou-kumiai-kyusai-ginkou-no setsuritsu-mo...*
invoke credit union relief bank GEN establishment
'the establishment of the invoking credit union relief bank'

(3) *shibunsyo-gizou-to gaikoku-jin-touroku-hou-ihan-no utagai-de*
private document falsification and foreigner registration law violation GEN suspicion INS
'on suspicion of the private document falsification and the violation of the foreigner registration law'

Figure 1: Example sentences.

entity recognition using a two-stage machine learning method. Different from previous work, this method regards a compound noun as a labeling unit (we call it *chunk*, hereafter), and estimates the labels of all the chunks in the *bunsetsu* using a machine learning method. In sentence (3), all the chunks in the second *bunsetsu* (i.e., "*gaikoku*", "*gaikoku-jin*", ···, "*gaikoku-jin-touroku-hou-ihan* ", ···, "*ihan*") are labeled, and in the case that the chunk "*gaikoku-jin-touroku-hou*" is labeled, the information about "*hou*" (law) is utilized in a natural manner. Then, in the *bunsetsu*, the best label assignment is determined. For example, among the combination of "*gaikoku-jin-touroku-hou*" (ARTIFACT) and "*ihan*" (OTHER), the combination of "*gaikoku-jin*" (PERSON) and "*touroku-hou-ihan*" (OTHER), etc., the best label assignment, "*gaikoku-jin-touroku-hou*" (ARTIFACT) and "*ihan*" (OTHER), is chosen based on a machine learning method. In this determination of the best label assignment, as the CKY parsing algorithm, the label assignment is determined by bottom-up dynamic programming. We conducted an experimental on CRL NE data, and achieved an F measure of 89.79, which is higher than previous work.

This paper is organized as follows. Section 2 reviews related work of NER, especially focusing on sequential labeling based method. Section 3 describes an overview of our proposed method. Section 4 presents two machine learning models, and Section 5 describes an analysis algorithm. Section 6 gives an experimental result.

2 Related Work

In Japanese Named Entity Recognition, the definition of Named Entity in IREX Workshop (IREX Committee, 1999) is usually used. In this definition, NEs are classified into eight classes: PERSON, LOCATION, ORGANIZATION, ARTIFACT, DATE, TIME, MONEY, and PERCENT. Table 1 shows example instances of each class.

class	example
PERSON	*Kimura Syonosuke*
LOCATION	*Taiheiyou* (Pacific Ocean)
ORGANIZATION	*Jimin-tou* (Liberal Democratic Party)
ARTIFACT	PL-*houan* (PL bill)
DATE	21-*seiki* (21 century)
TIME	*gozen-7-ji* (7 a.m.)
MONEY	500-*oku-en* (50 billions yen)
PERCENT	20 percent

Table 1: NE classes and their examples.

NER methods are divided into two approaches: rule-based approach and machine learning approach. According to previous work, machine learning approach achieved better performance than rule-based approach.

In general, a machine learning method is formalized as a sequential labeling problem. This problem is first assigning each token (character or morpheme) to several labels. In an SE-algorithm (Sekine et al., 1998), *S* is assigned to NE composed of one morpheme, *B, I, E* is assigned to the beginning, middle, end of NE, respectively, and *O* is assigned to the morpheme that is not an NE[2]. The labels S, B, I, and E are prepared for each NE classes, and thus the total number of labels is 33 (= 8 * 4 + 1).

The model for the label estimation is learned based on machine learning. The following features are generally utilized: characters, type of

[2]Besides, there are IOB1, IOB2 algorithm using only I,O,B and IOE1, IOE2 algorithm using only I,O,E (Kim and Veenstra, 1999).

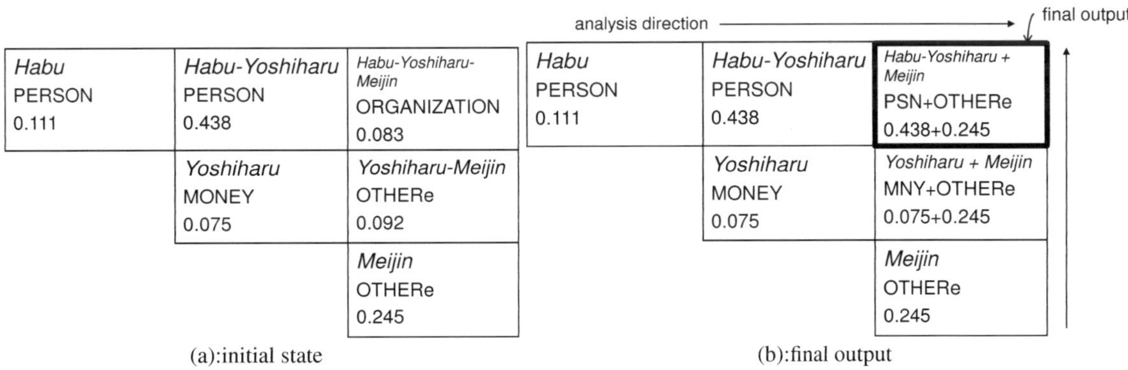

Figure 2: An overview of our proposed method. (the *bunsetsu* "*Habu-Yoshiharu-Meijin*")

character, POS, etc. about the morpheme and the surrounding two morphemes. The methods utilizing SVM or CRF are proposed.

Most of NER methods based on sequential labeling use only local information. Therefore, methods utilizing global information are proposed. Nakano et al. utilized as a feature the word sub class of NE on the analyzing direction in the *bunsetsu*, the noun in the end of the *bunsetsu* adjacent to the analyzing direction, and the head of each *bunsetsu* (Nakano and Hirai, 2004). Sasano et al. utilized cache feature, coreference result, syntactic feature, and caseframe feature as structural features (Sasano and Kurohashi, 2008).

Some work acquired knowledge from unannotated large corpus, and applied it to NER. Kazama et al. utilized a Named Entity dictionary constructed from Wikipedia and a noun clustering result obtained using huge amount of pairs of dependency relations (Kazama and Torisawa, 2008). Fukushima et al. acquired huge amount of category-instance pairs (e.g., "political party - New party DAICHI","company-TOYOTA") by some patterns from a large Web corpus (Fukushima et al., 2008).

In Japanese NER researches, CRL NE data are usually utilized for the evaluation. This data includes approximately 10 thousands sentences in news paper articles, in which approximately 20 thousands NEs are annotated. Previous work achieved an F measure of about 0.89 using this data.

3 Overview of Proposed Method

Our proposed method first estimates the label of all the compound nouns (chunk) in a *bunsetsu*. Then, the best label assignment is determined by bottom-up dynamic programming as the CKY parsing algorithm. Figure 2 illustrates an overview of our proposed method. In this example, the *bunsetsu* "*Habu-Yoshiharu-Meijin*" (Grand Master Yoshiharu Habu) is analyzed. First, the labels of all the chunks ("*Habu*", "*Habu-Yoshiharu*", "*Habu-Yoshiharu-Meijin*", $\cdots$, "*Meijin*", etc.) in the *bunsetsu* are analyzed using a machine learning method as shown in Figure 2 (a).

We call the state in Figure 2 (a) *initial state*, where the labels of all the chunks have been estimated. From this state, the best label assignment in the *bunsetsu* is determined. This procedure is performed from the lower left (corresponds to each morpheme) to the upper right like the CKY parsing algorithm as shown in Figure 2 (b). For example, when the label assignment for "*Habu-Yoshiharu*" is determined, the label assignment "*Habu-Yoshiharu*" (PERSON) and the label assignment "*Habu*" (PERSON) and "*Yoshiharu*" (OTHER) are compared, and the better one is chosen. While grammatical rules are utilized in a general CKY algorithm, this method chooses better label assignment for each cell using a machine learning method.

The learned models are the followings:

- the model that estimates the label of a chunk (*label estimation model*)
- the model that compares two label assignments (*label comparison model*)

The two models are described in detail in the next section.

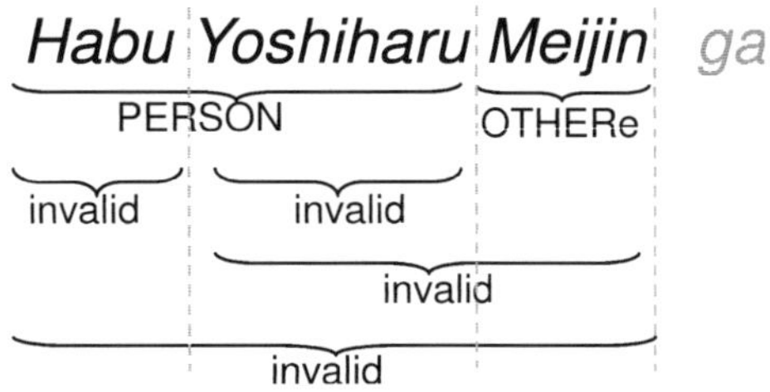

Figure 3: Label assignment for all the chunks in the *bunsetsu* "*Habu-Yoshiharu-Meijin*."

4 Model Learning

4.1 Label Estimation Model

This model estimates the label for each chunk. An analysis unit is basically *bunsetsu*. This is because 93.5% of named entities is located in a *bunsetsu* in CRL NE data. Exceptionally, the following expressions located in multiple *bunsetsus* tend to be an NE:

- expressions enclosed in parentheses (e.g., " '*Himeyuri-no tou*' " (The tower of Himeyuri) (ARTIFACT))
- expressions that have an entry in Wikipedia (e.g., "*Nihon-yatyou-no kai*" (Wild Bird Society of Japan) (ORGANIZATION))

Hereafter, *bunsetsu* is expanded when one of the above conditions meet. By this expansion, 98.6% of named entities is located in a *bunsetsu*[3].

For each *bunsetsu*, the head or tail function words are deleted. For example, in the *bunsetsu* "*Habu-Yoshiharu-Meijin-wa*", the tail function word "*wa*" (TOP) is deleted. In the *bunsetsu* "*yaku-san-bai*" (about three times), the head function word "*yaku*" (about) is deleted.

Next, for learning the label estimation model, all the chunks in a *bunsetsu* are attached to the correct label from a hand-annotated corpus. The label set is 13 classes, which includes eight NE class (as shown in Table 1), and five classes: OTHERs, OTHERb, OTHERi, OTHERe, and invalid.

The chunk that corresponds to a whole *bunsetsu* and does not contain any NEs is labeled as OTHERs, and the head, middle, tail chunk that does not correspond to an NE is labeled as OTHERb, OTHERi, OTHERe, respectively[4].

1. # of morphemes in the chunk
2. the position of the chunk in its *bunsetsu*
3. character type[5]
4. the combination of the character type of adjoining morphemes
   - For the chunk "Russian Army", this feature is "Katakana,Kanji"
5. word class, word sub class, and several features provided by a morphological analyzer JUMAN
6. several features[6] provided by a parser KNP
7. string of the morpheme in the chunk
8. IPADIC[7] feature
   - If the string of the chunk are registered in the following categories of IPADIC: "person", "location", "organization", and "general", this feature fires.
9. Wikipedia feature
   - If the string of the chunk has an entry in Wikipedia, this feature fires.
   - the hypernym extracted from its definition sentence using some patterns (e.g., The hypernym of "the Liberal Democratic Party" is a political party.)
10. cache feature
    - When the same string of the chunk appears in the preceding context, the label of the preceding chunk is used for the feature.
11. particles that the *bunsetsu* includes
12. the morphemes, particles, and head morpheme in the parent *bunsetsu*
13. the NE/category ratio in a case slot of predicate/noun case frame(Sasano and Kurohashi, 2008)
    - For example, in the case *ga* (NOM) of the predicate case frame "*kaiken*" (interview), the NE ratio "PERSON:0.245" is assigned to the case slot. Hence, in the sentence "*Habu-ga kaiken-shita*" (Mr. Habu interviewed), the feature "PERSON:0.245" is utilized for the chunk "*Habu*."
14. parenthesis feature
    - When the chunk in a parenthesis, this feature fires.

Table 2: Features for the label estimation model.

The chunk that is neither any eight NE class nor the above four OTHER is labeled as invalid.

In an example as shown in Figure 3, "*Habu-Yoshiharu*" is labeled as PERSON, "*Meijin*" is labeled as OTHERe, and the other chunks are labeled as invalid.

Next, the label estimation model is learned from the data in which the above label set is assigned

[3]As an example in which an NE is not included by an expanded *bunsetsu*, there are "*Toru-no Kimi*" (PERSON) and "*Osaka-fu midori-no kankyo-seibi-shitsu*" (ORGANIZATION).

[4]Each OTHER is assigned to the longest chunk that satisfies its condition in a chunk.

[5]The following five character types are considered: Kanji, Hiragana, Katakana, Number, and Alphabet.

[6]When a morpheme has an ambiguity, all the corresponding features fire.

[7]http://chasen.aist-nara.ac.jp/chasen/distribution.html.ja

to all the chunks. The features for the label estimation model are shown in Table 2. Among the features, as for feature (3), (5)–(8), three categories according to the position of a morpheme in the chunk are prepared: "head", "tail", and "anywhere." For example, in the chunk "*Habu-Yoshiharu-Meijin*," as for the morpheme "*Habu*", feature (7) is set to be "*Habu*" in "head" and as for the morpheme "*Yoshiharu*", feature (7) is set to be "*Yoshiharu*" in "anywhere."

The label estimation model is learned from pairs of label and feature in each chunk. To classify the multi classes, the one-vs-rest method is adopted (consequently, 13 models are learned). The SVM output is transformed by using the sigmoid function $\frac{1}{1+exp(-\beta x)}$, and the transformed value is normalized so that the sum of the value of 13 labels in a chunk is one.

The purpose for setting up the label "invalid" is as follows. In the chunk "*Habu*" and "*Yoshiharu*" in Figure 3, since the label "invalid" has a relatively higher score, the score of the label PERSON is relatively low. Therefore, when the label comparison described in Section 4.2 is performed, the label assignment "*Habu-Yoshiharu*" (PERSON) is likely to be chosen. In the chunk where the score of the label invalid has the highest score, the label that has the second highest score is adopted.

4.2 Label Comparison Model

This model compares the two label assignments for a certain string. For example, in the string "*Habu-Yoshiharu*", the model compares the following two label assignments:

- "*Habu-Yoshiharu*" is labeled as PERSON
- "*Habu*" is labeled as PERSON and "*Yoshiharu*" is labeled as MONEY

First, as shown in Figure 4, the two compared sets of chunks are lined up by sandwiching "**vs**." (The left one, right one is called the first set, the second set, respectively.) When the first set is correct, this example is positive: otherwise, this example is negative. The max number of chunks for each set is five, and thus examples in which the first or second set has more than five chunks are not utilized for the model learning.

Then, the feature is assigned to each example. The feature (13 dimensions) for each chunk is defined as follows: the first 12 dimensions are used

positive:
+1 *Habu-Yoshiharu* **vs** *Habu* + *Yoshiharu*
PSN PSN + MNY
+1 *Habu-Yoshiharu* + *Meijin* **vs** *Habu* + *Yoshiharu* + *Meijin*
PSN + OTHERe PSN + MONEY + OTHERe
⋮
negative:
- 1 *Habu-Yoshiharu-Meijin* **vs** *Habu-Yoshiharu* + *Meijin*
ORG PSN + OTHERe
⋮

Figure 4: Assignment of positive/negative examples.

for each label, which is estimated by the label estimation model, and the last 13th dimension is used for the score of an SVM output. Then, for the first and second set, the features for each chunk are arranged from the left, and zero vectors are placed in the remainder part.

Figure 5 illustrates the feature for "*Habu-Yoshiharu*" **vs** "*Habu* + *Yoshiharu*." The label comparison model is learned from such data using SVM. Note that only the fact that "*Habu-Yoshiharu*" is PERSON can be found from the hand-annotated corpus, and thus in the example "*Habu-Yoshiharu-Meijin*" **vs** "*Habu* + *Yoshiharu-Meijin*", we cannot determine which one is correct. Therefore, such example cannot be used for the model learning.

5 Analysis

First, the label of all the chunks in a *bunsetsu* is estimated by using the label estimation model described in Section 4.1. Then, the best label assignment in the *bunsetsu* is determined by applying the label comparison model described in Section 4.2 iteratively as shown in Figure 2 (b). In this step, the better label assignment is determined from bottom up as the CKY parsing algorithm.

For example, the initial state shown in Figure 2(a) is obtained using the label estimation model. Then, the label assignment is determined using the label comparison model from the lower left (corresponds to each morpheme) to the upper right. In determining the label assignment for the cell of "*Habu-Yoshiharu*" as shown in 6(a), the model compares the label assignment "B" with the label assignment "A+D." In this case, the model chooses the label assignment "B", that is, "*Habu - Yoshiharu*" is labeled as PERSON. Similarly, in determining the label assignment for the cell of "*Yoshiharu-Meijin*", the model compares the

chunk	*Habu-Yoshiharu*					*Habu*	*Yoshiharu*			
label	PERSON					PERSON	MONEY			
vector	$\mathbf{V_{11}}$	**0**	**0**	**0**	**0**	$\mathbf{V_{21}}$	$\mathbf{V_{22}}$	**0**	**0**	**0**

Figure 5: An example of the feature for the label comparison model. (The example is "*Habu-Yoshiharu* **vs** *Habu* + *Yoshiharu*", and $\mathbf{V_{11}}$, $\mathbf{V_{21}}$, $\mathbf{V_{22}}$, and **0** is a vector whose dimension is 13.)

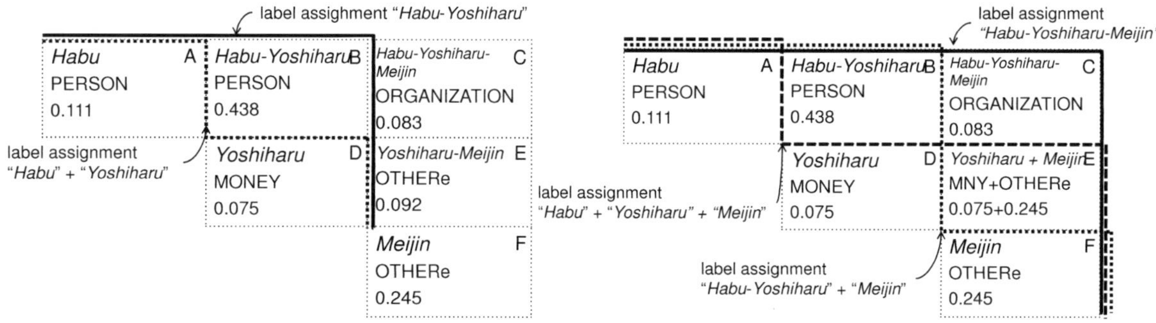

(a): label assignment for the cell "*Habu-Yoshiharu*". (b): label assignment for the cell "*Habu-Yoshiharu-Meijin*".

Figure 6: The label comparison model.

label assignment "E" with the label assignment "D+F." In this case, the model chooses the label assignment "D+F", that is, "*Yoshiharu*" is labeled as MONEY and "*Meijin*" is labeled as OTHERe. When the label assignment consists of multiple chunks, the content of the cell is updated. In this case, the cell "E" is changed from "*Yoshiharu-Meijin*" (OTHERe) to "*Yoshiharu* + *Meijin*" (MONEY + OTHERe).

As shown in Figure 6(b), in determining the best label assignment for the upper right cell, that is, the final output is determined, the model compares the label assignment "A+D+F", "B+F", and "C". When there are more than two candidates of label assignments for a cell, all the label assignments are compared in a pairwise, and the label assignment that obtains the highest score is adopted.

In the label comparing step, the label assignment in which OTHER_* follows OTHER_* (OTHER_* - OTHER_*) is not allowed since each OTHER is assigned to the longest chunk as described in Section 4.1. When the first combination of chunks equals to the second combination of chunks, the comparison is not performed.

6 Experiment

To demonstrate the effectiveness of our proposed method, we conducted an experiment on CRL NE data. In this data, 10,718 sentences in 1,174 news articles are annotated with eight NEs. The expression to which it is difficult to annotate manually is labeled as OPTIONAL, and was not used for both

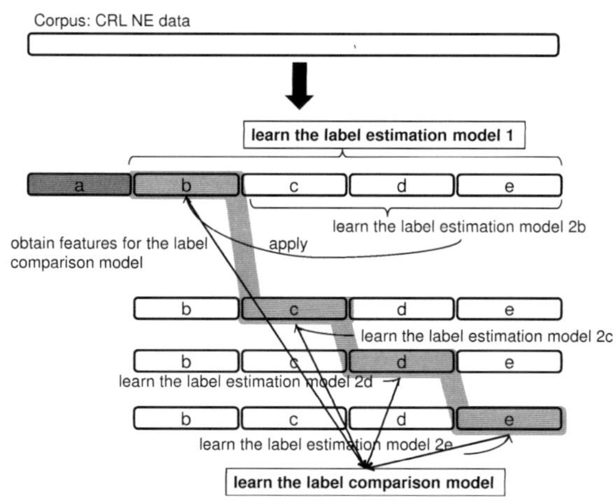

Figure 7: 5-fold cross validation.

the model learning[8] and the evaluation.

We performed 5-fold cross validation following previous work. Different from previous work, our work has to learn the SVM models twice. Therefore, the corpus was divided as shown in Figure 7. Let us consider the analysis in the part (a). First, the label estimation model 1 is learned from the part (b)-(e). Then, the label estimation model 2b is learned from the part (c)-(e), and applying the learned model to the part (b), features for learning the label comparison model are obtained. Similarly, the label estimation model 2c is learned from the part (b),(d),(e), and applying it to the part (c), features are obtained. It is the same with the part

[8]Exceptionally, "OPTIONAL" is used when the label estimation model for OTHER_* and invalid is learned.

	Recall	Precision
ORGANIZATION	81.83 (3008/3676)	88.37 (3008/3404)
PERSON	90.05 (3458/3840)	93.87 (3458/3684)
LOCATION	91.38 (4992/5463)	92.44 (4992/5400)
ARTIFACT	46.72 (349/ 747)	74.89 (349/ 466)
DATE	93.27 (3327/3567)	93.12 (3327/3573)
TIME	88.25 (443/ 502)	90.59 (443/ 489)
MONEY	93.85 (366/ 390)	97.60 (366/ 375)
PERCENT	95.33 (469/ 492)	95.91 (469/ 489)
ALL-SLOT	87.87	91.79
F-measure		89.79

Table 3: Experimental result.

(d) and (e). Then, the label comparison model is learned from the obtained features. After that, the analysis in the part (a) is performed by using both the label estimation model 1 and the label comparison model.

In this experiment, a Japanese morphological analyzer, JUMAN[9], and a Japanese parser, KNP[10] were adopted. The two SVM models were learned with polynomial kernel of degree 2, and β in the sigmoid function was set to be 1.

Table 6 shows an experimental result. An F-measure in all NE classes is 89.79.

7 Discussion

7.1 Comparison with Previous Work

Table 7 presents the comparison with previous work, and our method outperformed previous work. Among previous work, Fukushima et al. acquired huge amount of category-instance pairs (e.g., "political party - New party DAICHI","company-TOYOTA") by some patterns from a large Web corpus, and Sasano et al. utilized the analysis result of corefer resolution as a feature for the model learning. Therefore, in our method, by incorporating these knowledge and/or such analysis result, the performance would be improved.

Compared with Sasano et al., our method achieved the better performance in analyzing a long compound noun. For example, in the *bunsetsu* "*Oushu-tsuujyou-senryoku-sakugen-jyouyaku*" (Treaty on Conventional Armed Forces in Europe), while Sasano et al. labeled "*Oushu*" (Europe) as LOCATION, our method correctly labeled "*Oushu-tsuujyou-senryoku-sakugen-jyouyaku*" as ARTIFACT. Sasano et al. incorrectly labeled "*Oushu*" as LOCATION although they utilized the information about the head of *bunsetsu* "*jyouyaku*" (treaty). In our method, for the cell "*Oushu*", invalid has the highest score, and thus the score of LOCATION relatively drops. Similarly, for the cell "*senryoku-sakugen-jyouyaku*", invalid has the highest score. Consequently, "*Oushu-tsuujyou-senryoku-sakugen-jyouyaku*" is correctly labeled as ARTIFACT.

In the *bunsetsu* "*gaikoku-jin-touroku-hou-ihan*" (the violation of the foreigner registration law), while Sasano et al. labeled "*touroku-hou*" as ARTIFACT, our method correctly labeled "*gaikoku-jin-touroku-hou*" as ARTIFACT. Sasano et al. cannot utilize the information about "*hou*" that is useful for the label estimation since the head of this *bunsetsu* is "*ihan*." In contrast, in estimating the label of the chunk "*gaikoku-jin-touroku-hou*", the information of "*hou*" can be utilized.

7.2 Error Analysis

There were some errors in analyzing a Katakana alphabet word. In the following example, although the correct is that "Batistuta" is labeled as PERSON, the system labeled it as OTHERs.

(4) Italy-*de* *katsuyaku-suru* Batistuta-*wo*
Italy LOC active Batistuta ACC

kuwaeta Argentine
call Argentine

'Argentine called Batistuta who was active in Italy.'

There is not an entry of "Batistuta" in the dictionary of JUMAN nor Wikipedia, and thus only the surrounding information is utilized. However, the case analysis of "*katsuyaku*" (active) is incorrect, which leads to the error of "Batistuta".

There were some errors in applying the label comparison model although the analysis of each chunk is correct. For example, in the *bunsetsu* "HongKong-*seityou*" (Government of HongKong), the correct is that "HongKong-*seityou*" is labeled as ORGANIZATION. As shown in Figure 8 (b), the system incorrectly labeled "HongKong" as LOCATION. As shown in Figure 8(a), although in the initial state, "HongKong-*seityou*" was correctly labeled as ORGANIZATION, the label assignment "HongKong + *seityou*" was incorrectly chosen by the label comparison model. To cope with this problem, we are planning to the adjustment of the value β in the sigmoid function and the refinement of the

[9]http://nlp.kuee.kyoto-u.ac.jp/nl-resource/juman-e.html
[10]http://nlp.kuee.kyoto-u.ac.jp/nl-resource/knp-e.html

	F1	analysis unit	distinctive features
(Fukushima et al., 2008)	89.29	character	Web
(Kazama and Torisawa, 2008)	88.93	character	Wikipedia,Web
(Sasano and Kurohashi, 2008)	89.40	morpheme	structural information
(Nakano and Hirai, 2004)	89.03	character	*bunsetsu* feature
(Masayuki and Matsumoto, 2003)	87.21	character	
(Isozaki and Kazawa, 2003)	86.77	morpheme	
proposed method	**89.79**	compound noun	Wikipedia,structural information

Table 4: Comparison with previous work. (All work was evaluated on CRL NE data using cross validation.)

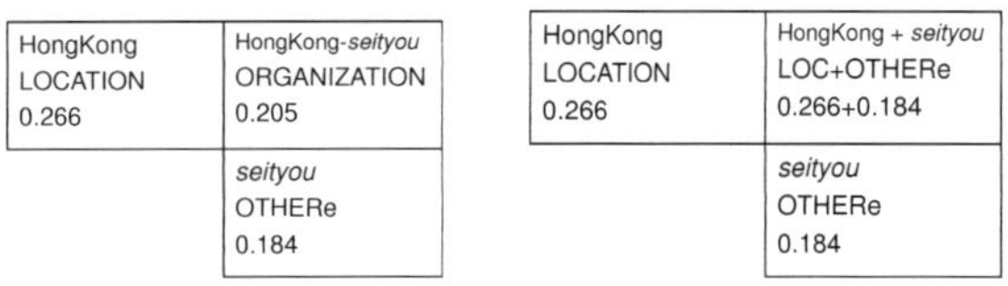

(a):initial state (b):the final output

Figure 8: An example of the error in the label comparison model.

features for the label comparison model.

8 Conclusion

This paper proposed bottom-up Named Entity Recognition using a two-stage machine learning method. This method first estimates the label of all the chunks in a *bunsetsu* using a machine learning, and then the best label assignment is determined by bottom-up dynamic programming. We conducted an experiment on CRL NE data, and achieved an F-measure of 89.79.

We are planning to integrate this method with the syntactic and case analysis method (Kawahara and Kurohashi, 2007), and perform syntactic, case, and Named Entity analysis simultaneously to improve the overall accuracy.

References

Ken'ichi Fukushima, Nobuhiro Kaji, and Masaru Kitsuregawa. 2008. Use of massive amounts of web text in Japanese named entity recognition. In *Proceedings of Data Engineering Workshop (DEWS2008)*. A3-3 (in Japanese).

IREX Committee, editor. 1999. *Proceedings of the IREX Workshop*.

Hideki Isozaki and Hideto Kazawa. 2003. Speeding up support vector machines for named entity recognition. *Transaction of Information Processing Society of Japan*, 44(3):970–979. (in Japanese).

Daisuke Kawahara and Sadao Kurohashi. 2007. Probabilistic coordination disambiguation in a fully-lexicalized Japanese parser. In *Proceedings of the 2007 Joint Conference on Empirical Methods in Natural Language Processing and Computational Natural Language Learning (EMNLP-CoNLL2007)*, pages 304–311.

Jun'ichi Kazama and Kentaro Torisawa. 2008. Inducing gazetteers for named entity recognition by large-scale clustering of dependency relations. In *Proceedings of ACL-08: HLT*, pages 407–415.

Erik F. Tjong Kim and Jorn Veenstra. 1999. Representing text chunks. In *Proceedings of EACL '99*, pages 173–179.

Vajay Krishnan and Christopher D.Manning. 2006. An effective two-stage model for exploiting non-local dependencies in named entity recognition. pages 1121–1128.

John Lafferty, Andrew McCallun, and Fernando Pereira. 2001. Conditional random fields: Probabilistic models for segmenting and labeling sequence data. In *Proceedings of the Eighteenth International Conference (ICML'01)*, pages 282–289.

Asahara Masayuki and Yuji Matsumoto. 2003. Japanese named entity extraction with redundant morphological analysis. In *Proceeding of HLT-NAACL 2003*, pages 8–15.

Keigo Nakano and Yuzo Hirai. 2004. Japanese named entity extraction with bunsetsu features. *Transaction of Information Processing Society of Japan*, 45(3):934–941. (in Japanese).

Ryohei Sasano and Sadao Kurohashi. 2008. Japanese named entity recognition using structural natural language processing. In *Proceeding of Third International Joint Conference on Natural Language Processing*, pages 607–612.

Satoshi Sekine, Ralph Grishman, and Hiroyuki Shinnou. 1998. A decision tree method for finding and classifying names in japanese texts. In *Proceedings of the Sixth Workshop on Very Large Corpora (WVLC-6)*, pages 171–178.

Vladimir Vapnik. 1995. *The Nature of Statistical Learning Theory*. Springer.

Abbreviation Generation for Japanese Multi-Word Expressions

Hiromi Wakaki[†] **Hiroko Fujii**[†] **Masaru Suzuki**[†]
Mika Fukui[†] **Kazuo Sumita**[†]
[†]Toshiba Corporation
1 Komukai-Toshiba, Saiwai-ku, Kawasaki, 212-8582, Japan
{hiromi.wakaki, hiroko.fujii, masaru1.suzuki,
mika.fukui, kazuo.sumita}@toshiba.co.jp

Abstract

This paper proposes a novel method for generating Japanese abbreviations from their full forms with the Log-Linear Model (LLM) in order to take advantage of characteristic patterns of Japanese abbreviation. Our experimental results show that the method is effective for TV program titles that contain colloquial expressions. The proposed method achieved 78.8% recall for the top 30 candidates, whereas a baseline method using Conditional Random Fields (CRFs) achieved 68.3% recall. Moreover, from the results of experiments using six data sets classified according to types of character and semantic categories, we show that each performance of the above two methods depends on the types of the full forms.

1 Introduction

Much research has been done on abbreviation extraction to detect terms having the same meaning. However, most previous studies (Hisamitsu and Niwa, 2001; Park and Byrd, 2001; Schwartz and Hearst, 2003; Adar, 2004; Sakai and Masuyama, 2005; Nadeau and Turney, 2005; Okazaki and Ananiadou, 2006; Okazaki et al., 2008(1); Okazaki et al., 2008(2)) aimed at extracting abbreviations of organization names and technical terms from well-written documents such as news articles and techincal papers.

Many Japanese terms indicating individual TV programs, songs, comics, novels, and so on, are multi-word expressions and have the characteristics distinct from terms treated in most previous studies on abbreviation extraction. These terms can take several grammatical forms: a noun phrase, a sentence fragment, and even a sentence. Also, many of these expressions contain a variety of types of characters: kanji, hiragana, katakana, alphabet, digit, and symbol, and some of them contain colloquial expressions[1]. Abbreviations of these expressions are often used in colloquial text such as chat or blog, and spoken sentences. To treat an abbreviation as a term having the same meaning as the original expression for NLP applications such as keyboard-based and speech-based information retrieval, an abbreviation generation method effective for this type of multi-word expressions is needed. However, it is not easy to ascertain abbreviations associated with their full forms. This is because although these terms become widely used in speech, they do not appear in well-written documents, such as newspaper articles or research papers, in which the abbreviations are clearly defined for use in the subsequent texts with certain lexical patterns, such as parenthesis. Therefore this paper describes an approach to generate abbreviation candidates from an original term and to rank them according to their probabilities of abbreviation. We assume that top-ranked abbreviations will be narrowed down by using Web search results in the future.

2 Japanese Abbreviation

2.1 Data Sets

Transformations into abbreviations are strongly dependent on languages. For instance, the term "ファミリーレストラン (family restaurant)" is abbreviated as "ファミレス (famires)" in Japanese, whereas English speakers do not abbreviate it in the same way as Japanese do. To investigate Japanese abbreviations, we collected them from different perspectives, that is, types of character and semantic categories. Table 1 shows abbreviation data types, their word counts, and so on. Ex-

[1]TV program titles contain colloquial expressions such as slang, pun, coined words, and dialect. For example, in well-written documents, we do not see such a expression as "I'm Not An Errand Boy!" showed in Figure 2.

Proceedings of the 2009 Workshop on Multiword Expressions, ACL-IJCNLP 2009, pages 63–70,
Suntec, Singapore, 6 August 2009. ©2009 ACL and AFNLP

amples are given in Figure 2 at the end of this paper.

We extracted abbreviations listed and described on the Japanese Wikipedia site [2], which is a multilingual project to create a complete and accurate open content encyclopedia. First, we collected lists of abbreviations classified according to types of Japanese character. Japanese has three original types of character: kanji, katakana, and hiragana. Other types of character are used, such as alphabets, numbers, and symbols. However, hiragana is mainly used with kanji, and numbers and symbols are used with other characters. Therefore, we used three abbreviation lists classified according to alphabetical words [3], katakana words [4], and kanji words with hiragana[5](Figure 2) on Wikipedia. We extracted pairs of abbreviations and their full forms from each list and obtained 928, 245, and 399 abbreviations, respectively.

Also, we extracted pairs of university names and their abbreviations from a list of university abbreviations on Wikipedia [6]. In Japanese, many names of organizations have a noun phrase structure combining several nouns, such as names of places ("日本 (Japan)", "東京 (Tokyo)"), names of fields ("医科 (medical)", "科学 (science)"), for whom ("女子 (female)"), and the type of organization("大学 (university)", "研究所"(research laboratory)). Therefore, we used names of universities and extracted 523 abbreviations. Almost all of the nouns are kanji.

Additionally, we extracted abbreviations of TV program titles from descriptions on each page of Wikipedia. This is because many TV program titles contain various types of characters or colloquial expressions different from the others we extracted. However, there are no lists of TV program titles in Wikipedia. Therefore, we gathered TV program titles satisfying the following criterion: the first sentence of the description of the Wikipedia page of the TV program title indicates that the page is about the TV program. And, in the same paragraph, if abbreviations are introduced by using key phrases such as "略語は A"(it means "it is abbreviated as A"), we extracted bold or parenthetical words in the key phrases. There were 326 abbreviations.

Finally, we gathered abbreviations of TV program titles in TV schedules written in short form because of space limitations. In this process, we used program titles in TV schedules in newspapers as short forms and EPG [7] data as long forms. When a title in the schedule is written with short form of the title with the same date, time, and channel as EPG data, we recognized that it is an abbreviation and the other is its full form. We extracted 603 abbreviations.

2.2 Characteristics

In this paper, we focus on abbreviations that lack some characters compared with the full forms. The followings are well-known characteristics of Japanese abbreviations (Sakai and Masuyama, 2005; Enoki et al., 2007; Murayama and Okumura, 2008). Abbreviations are created according to rules: (1) retain the beginning of a word and omit the rest (truncation); (2) divide an original term into base words, retaining several substrings from some of them, and combine them (contraction). In particular, four-mora[8] katakana abbreviations are often created by combining two-mora as in the case of the katakana words in Figure 2. Also, the length of an abbreviation in kanji tends to be two or three letters as in the case of the kanji words in Figure 2. Moreover, if an original term consists of katakana with the specific characters such as sokuon [9] and chōn[10] in the middle, these characters tend to be dropped in abbreviations. The second and third of katakana terms in Figure 2 are an example of this.

3 Proposed Method

In this section, we propose a new method to generate Japanese abbreviations by using the Log-Linear Model to rank abbreviation candidates. As mentioned in Section 2.2, Japanese abbreviation characteristics are evident in the composition of abbreviations, not in generation rules from their full forms. Therefore, we first generate possible abbreviations from an original term and rank them in descending order of probability of abbreviations. Our method uses a three-step process as

[2]http://ja.wikipedia.org/wiki/

[3]http://ja.wikipedia.org/wiki/欧文略語一覧

[4]http://ja.wikipedia.org/wiki/カタカナ略語一覧

[5]http://ja.wikipedia.org/wiki/漢字略語一覧

[6]http://ja.wikipedia.org/wiki/大学の略称

[7]EPG (Electronic Program Guide) broadcast on some multiplexes that provide detailed information about programs in an upcoming week on some stations.

[8]The minimal unit of a syllable.

[9]Sokuon is written as "ッ" in katakana and "っ" in hiragana to show a geminate consonant

[10]Chōn, is written as "—" to show a long vowel.

Class	Type	NT	Average number of characters								SC(%)
		(#)	Av	SD	(a)	(b)	(c)	(d)	(e)	(f)	
Character type	Alpha.	928	23.5	9.0	0.0	0.0	0.0	**21.4**	0.0	2.1	100.0
	Kata.	245	8.8	3.1	0.4	**8.0**	0.3	0.0	0.0	0.2	79.2
	Kanji	399	6.3	3.8	**5.9**	0.3	0.2	0.0	0.0	0.0	91.0
Semantic category	Univ.	523	6.0	1.4	**6.0**	0.0	0.0	0.0	0.0	0.0	98.1
	TV1	326	10.5	5.6	3.1	**3.6**	2.1	1.2	0.3	0.3	28.8
	TV2	603	10.9	4.2	1.6	**4.5**	2.6	1.7	0.1	0.4	19.1

Table 1: Abbreviation data sets, their types and number of terms(NT), average number of characters with standard deviation(SD), average number of characters per term in each type of character((a)kanji, (b)katakana, (c)hiragana, (d)alphabet, (e)number, (f)space), and proportion of terms with a single type of character (SC).

follows: 1)base word division, 2)candidate generation, and 3)ranking abbreviations.

3.1 Step1: Base Word Division

In this step, we divide terms into base words for abbreviations because Japanese is an agglutinative language. In order to deal with neologisms and colloquial expressions, we divide terms by using web search results instead of morphological analyzer.

When a term t is divided into two substrings after the ith charcter t, we denote the anterior half by $s_{i,ant}$ and the posterior half by $s_{i,post}$. A link strength $D(t_i)$ between $s_{i,ant}$ and $s_{i,post}$ is defined as follows:

$$D(t_i) = \frac{hit(s)}{min(hit(s_{i,ant}), hit(s_{i,post}))}$$

Note that hit(t) is calculated as the number of search results by using the term t in double quotes as one query on the Web[11]. The formulation of $D(t_i)$ is mostly the same as Simpson's Coefficient except that the numerator is modified. We divide the term t after the kth character where $D(t_k)$ is the smallest and repeat this process by using substrings divided in the previous operation as new t_is recursively. We heuristically set the stopping conditions as two kanji characters or four characters of other types. This dividing process works well because a set of words containing a term is stylized expression that is different from a sentence.

For example, suppose that a term t is "VivaVivaV6", which is one of the TV program titles. All divisions into two of the term are "V/ivaVivaV6", "Vi/vaVivaV6", $\cdots$, and "VivaVivaV/6". Here, the symbol "/"" indicates a division point. Then, $D(t_i)$s are calculated as follows:

$$D(t_1) = \frac{hit(\text{“VivaVivaV6”})}{min(hit(\text{“V”}), hit(\text{“ivaVivaV6”}))}$$

$$\vdots$$

$$D(t_9) = \frac{hit(\text{“VivaVivaV6”})}{min(hit(\text{“VivaVivaV”}), hit(\text{“6”}))}$$

When $D(t_8)$ is the smallest of all $D(t_i)$, "VivaVivaV6" is divided into "VivaViva" and "V6". The length of "V6" is two and is satisfied with the stopping conditions. Then, we continue to calculate $D(t_i)$ of "VivaViva" because the length of the substring is not satisfied with the stopping conditions.

Finally, the divisions are fixed based on the following modifications. If a division is just before the sokuon or the chōn, we eliminate the division because these cannot appear at the beginning of a word. Also, if the division is just before "の"(no), which is a hiragana character and one of the particles used to indicate possession and so on, we insert a division after the "の"(no) to make it one word because of the stopping conditions. Additionally, we combine some segments to form one word when there is a word in a transliteration dictionary of katakana corresponding to an English word.

3.2 Step2:Candidate Generation

In this step, we generate abbreviation candidates by applying the following simple rules to all words containing a certain term. These rules are based on the Japanese abbreviation characteristics described in Section 2.2.

1) Do not use this word
2) Use this word in full
3) Use the first character of this word

[11]. We used Yahoo web search API. http://developer.yahoo.co.jp/search/web/V1/webSearch.html

4) Use the first two characters of this word
5) Use the first three characters of this word
6) Drop sokuon and chōn, and do 4)
7) Drop sokuon and chōn, and do 5)
All rules are applied to all words divided by the process in step 1. For example, in the case of "Viva/Viva/V6", all rules are used for "Viva", "Viva", and "V6". Then, if 3), 3), 2) are used for each base word, we get a candidate "VVV6". With the rules, we can get all candidates combining substrings at the beginning of each word because we used the stop conditions of character length of less than four in step 1. However, note that we use mora instead of character in the case of phonographic characters. Also, we eliminate duplicative candidates.

3.3 Step3: Ranking Abbreviations

LLM is a probabilistic model widely used as a maximum entropy model for many NLP tasks (Manning and Schutze, 1999). We use standard LLM to rank the abbreviations.

Consider a set of observations x for each sample of an object or event with y. Log-Linear Model gives a probability $p(y|x;\lambda)$ of an event by representing an event y as features $f_j(x_l, y_k)$.

$$p(y|x;\lambda) = \frac{1}{Z(x,\lambda)} \exp(\Sigma_j \lambda_j f_j(x,y)) \quad (1)$$

Here, $\lambda_j (j = 1, ..., M)$ or α_j is a model parameter, and it represents the weight of a feature $f_j(x_l, y_k)$. Also, regularization term $Z(x,\lambda)$ is calculated as follows:

$$Z(x,\lambda) = \Sigma_{y' \in Y(x)} \exp(\Sigma_j \lambda_j f_j(x,y'))$$

Note that $Y(x)$ represents a set of output y corresponding to x. The numerator of the Formula (1) is the same as the following by replacing e^{λ_j} as α_j.

$$\begin{aligned} s(x,y,\lambda) &= \exp(\Sigma_j \lambda_j f_j(x,y)) \\ &= \alpha_1^{f_1(x,y)} \alpha_2^{f_2(x,y)} \cdots \alpha_M^{f_M(x,y)} \quad (2) \end{aligned}$$

We formalize the abbreviation generation task as a ranking problem in which the probability $p(y|x;\lambda)$ of abbreviation y in a given set $Y(x)$ of abbreviation candidates is modeled when its full form x is observed. For example, assume that you assign a full form "VivavivaV6" to x. The set $Y(x)$ contains abbreviation candidates generated from the full form in Step2 such as "VVV6", "VivaV", "ViVi", and so on. We used Amis implementation [12] for Log-Linear Model.

1) **Features**
We use the features below for the Japanese abbreviation characteristics with letter length and so on as mentioned in the Section 2.2. We denote a substring of a ith base word containing an abbreviation candidate by sub_i $(i = 1, \cdots, m)$, where m is the total number of base words. Then, let $ch(sub_i)$ denote letter type of character of sub_i, and let $len(sub_i)$ denote length of sub_i. Additionally, let $sum(len(sub_i), 1, m)$ denote a summation of $len(sub_i)(i = 1, \cdots, m)$, and let $com((f_1(i), f_2(i)), 1, m)$ denote a combination of a feature $f_1(i)$ and a feature $f_2(i)$ from $i = 1$ to $i = m$. Here, we show all categories of features we used as follows:.

- $tp = com((ch(sub_i, len(sub_i))), 1, m)$
- $tl = com((ch(sub_i)), 1, m)$
- $e = com((len(sub_i)), 1, m)$
- $w = sub_i$ $(i = 1, \cdots, m)$
- $ab = sum(len(sub_i), 1, m)$
- $enum = m$

A substring of a ith base word is generated by applying one of the rules from 2) to 7) in Step 2. However, when an abbreviation candidate corresponds to one substring of its full form, we set its base word to the candidate itself even if the candidate was generated by combining some substrings.

Table 2 shows features for "VVV6" whose original term is "VivaVivaV6". Its base words sub_i are "V", "V", and "V6" because of the division as "V/V/V6". When $i = 1$, $ch(sub_1)$ is equal to ALPHA, that is, an alphabetical character, and $len(sub_1)$ is equal to 1. Therefore, for "VVV6", a feature in a category tp is generated by combination of the $ch(sub_i)$ and $len(sub_i)$ from $i = 1$ to $i = m$, that is, 1ALPHA_1ALPHA_2ALPHA. Other features are also generated by calculating in the same way as tp.

We cannot list all possible features because they depend on compositions of abbreviation candidates. Therefore, we prepare a $zero$ feature for each category. If features do not appear in positive examples in a training data set, we assign them to $zero$ features. For example, because a feature "1KANJI_5KANJI" in category "tp" does not appear in positive examples of a training set, we use

[12] http://www-tsujii.is.s.u-tokyo.ac.jp/amis/

Category	Feature
tp	1ALPHA_1ALPHA_2ALPHA
tl	ALPHA_ALPHA_ALPHA
e	1_1_2
w	V, V, V6
ab	ab4
enum	enum3

Table 2: Features for abbreviation "V/V/V6" whose full form is "Viva/Viva/V6".

"tp0" as an alternative feature. However, $w0$ is assigned when any features in category "w" do not appear in them.

We assign l_1 to a set of all features that appear in positive examples in a training data set, such as 1ALPHA_1ALPHA_2ALPHA, 1_1_2, V, V, V6, ab4. We also assign l_0 to a set of $zero$ features, i.e. tp0, tl0, e0, w0, ab0, enum0. Then, let L denote a set merged l_1 and l_0.

2) **Training and Test**

First, we obtain the above-mentioned feature set L with a training data set. Next, these features are assigned to all abbreviation candidates generated from the training data set in step 2. Then, a parameter α_j ($j = 1, \cdots, |L|$) of the Log-Linear Model is calculated by using Amis. Finally, the probabilities of all abbreviation candidates generated from a test data in step 2 are calculated by the Formula (2).

4 Evaluation

4.1 Baseline Method

CRFs (Lafferty et al., 2001) are Log-Linear Models, which are often used for the labeling or parsing of sequential data and are widely applied for many NLP tasks. Some researchers already used CRFs for abbreviation extraction (Okazaki et al., 2008(1)) or generation (Saikou et al., 2008). Therefore, we evaluate a method using CRFs as a baseline.

We formalize the abbreviation generation task as a sequence labeling problem in which each letter contained in an original term is to be used in its abbreviation[13] (Fig. 1). We also designed features attached to each character: morpheme word containing the letter, reading of the morpheme word, type of character, the first character or not in the morpheme word, the first character or not in the segment, and so on. We used MeCab[14] as a morphological analysis and CRF++ implementation [15] for CRFs.

[13] In (Saikou et al., 2008), they formalized the abbreviation generation task as a sequence labeling problem in which each mora contained in a term is to be used in its abbreviation. To avoid reading estimation, we generate abbreviations by abbreviating their original characters.

	Label	Features				
	-	word	reading	POS	Head of word	
朝	○	朝	ちょー	Noun	1	・・・
は	×	は	わ	Particle	1	・・・
ビ	○	ビタミン	びたみん	Noun	1	・・・
タ	○	ビタミン	びたみん	Noun	0	・・・
ミ	×	ビタミン	びたみん	Noun	0	・・・
ン	×	ビタミン	びたみん	Noun	0	・・・

Figure 1: Feature examples of CRFs and values for the abbreviation "朝ビタ (asabita)" whose formal form is "朝はビタミン (asa wa bitamin)".

4.2 Results and Discussion

We evaluate recall in the top 1, 5, 10, 30, and 50 abbreviation candidates generated with both the proposed method and the baseline method on the six data sets. The performance is measured under a ten-fold cross-validation where the parameters are fine-tuned in the top 30 in the training procedure.

Table 3 shows recall with the baseline method. Table 4 shows recall, and the bottom row in the table shows differences between recall with CRFs and that with proposed method in the top 30.

In the top 30, recall in Table 3 of alphabetical words, names of universities, and kanji words are 99.1%, 97.9%, and 92.5% respectively. From the point of view of types of character, most of these are composed of a single type of character as shown in column SC of Table 1. In contrast, recall in Table 3 of TV program titles 1 and 2 are 68.3% and 80.9% respectively. These results are much lower than the others. As a result of applying our method, Table 4 showed that recall of TV program titles improved 10.5% compared with the baseline method. This is because the method using CRFs cannot use the features of generated abbreviations since it is an approach to decide whether each character of an original form is to be used in its abbreviation. It seems that this leads to the disadvantages of generating abbreviations of TV program titles containing various types of character and colloquial expressions. However, there

[14] http://mecab.sourceforge.net/

[15] http://crfpp.sourceforge.net/

Recall@n	Alphabet	Katakana	Kanji	Univ.	TV1	TV2
1	89.1%	29.4%	47.9%	19.9%	11.1%	9.3%
5	97.0%	67.3%	71.7%	80.9%	37.5%	45.8%
10	98.4%	77.1%	81.5%	92.9%	48.6%	62.5%
30	99.1%	89.0%	92.5%	97.9%	68.3%	80.9%
50	99.4%	93.9%	94.7%	98.9%	73.8%	86.9%

Table 3: Recall in the top 1, 5, 10, 30, and 50 abbreviation candidates generated with CRFs.

Recall@n	Alphabet	Katakana	Kanji	Univ.	TV1	TV2
1	87.4%	36.3%	39.1%	33.5%	19.9%	20.2%
5	92.2%	66.5%	65.2%	71.5%	48.2%	42.8%
10	93.0%	81.6%	73.9%	84.9%	61.3%	59.2%
30	94.1%	91.0%	85.2%	92.5%	78.8%	81.1%
50	94.4%	92.7%	86.7%	93.3%	85.3%	85.4%
all	95.6%	94.7%	90.4%	94.8%	93.9%	90.3%
Differences(Recall@30)	−5.1%	+2.0%	−7.3%	−5.4%	+10.5%	+0.2%

Table 4: Recall in the top 1, 5, 10, 30, and 50 abbreviation candidates generated with the proposed method, and differences between the recall with CRFs and that with the proposed method in the top 30.

is little difference of recall between the baseline and the proposed method for the TV program titles 2. This is because most of the TV program titles 2 were systematically created by simple rules such as getting the initial several letters that satisfy space limitations.

On the other hand, recall of the proposed method for alphabetical words, kanji words, and names of universities was -5.1%, -7.3%, -5.4% lower, respectively, than in the case of using the baseline method. This is because some abbreviations could not be generated by the given generation rules and, as can be seen in Table 4, recall of these data sets peaks. From these results, we conclude that the baseline method is suited to a term containing a single type of character such as alphabetical words and kanji words, whereas the proposed method is suited to a term containing multiple types of character.

When we used the division in step 2 as an alternative to MeCab, recall with CRFs differed approximately less than $\pm 1\%$ from recall in Table 3. On the other hand, when we used MeCab as an alternative to the division in step 2, recall with the proposed method was significantly lower than in Table 4.

We cannot compare our performance directly with the previous work because of the differences in data sets. For reference, Murayama et al. (2006) reported 68.4% recall in the top 30 with the Noisy-Channel Model. They used 851 abbreviations corresponding to 748 full forms extracted from Wikipedia. Saikou et al. (2008) reported 72.5% recall in the top 30 with CRFs. They used 51 abbreviations collected by WoZ[16] as test data and 781 abbreviations that appeared in Wikipedia as training data.

4.3 Combination of two methods

Table 4 shows that the baseline method is better for the alphabetical words, names of universities, and kanji words, whereas the proposed method is better for others. However the classification on Table 1 is made by hand. Here, we automatically classified them into the following case A and B based on the conditions according to types of character after merging the six data sets in Table 1. Then, we applied the method with CRFs to the case A and the proposed method to the case B.

Case A is when an original term is (1) an alphabetical term with more than two words, (2) a kanji term in which other characters do not constitute, or (3) a term of (1) or (2) with numerals or symbols. Case B is when an original term does not fulfill the conditions of the case A.

The total number of abbreviations was 3114 (1921 in the case A and 1103 in the case B). Ta-

[16] Wizard-of-Oz

ble 5 shows the number of abbreviations in each case for each data set. The total performance was measured by calculating weighted average for two recall scores, that is, in the case of A and B measured under a ten-fold cross-validation in the top 30. As a result, recall was 97.1% and 76.9% in the case A and B respectively, and the total recall was 89.4%. Additionally, we conducted an experiment in which the method with CRFs was applied to all the abbreviations as a baseline. The recall was 87.0% measured under a ten-fold cross-validation in the top 30. The results show that it is better to apply different methods according to types of character than to apply one method to the entire data set.

5 Conclusion

In this paper, we proposed a method for generating Japanese abbreviations from their full forms with LLM. As a result of experiments, the proposed method was confirmed to be effective for TV program titles. It achieved 78.8% recall in the top 30, and improved 10.5% from a baseline method using CRFs that achieved 68.3% recall. We also described difficulties in generating Japanese abbreviations by examining six data sets classified according to types of character and semantic categories. Consequently, we showed that the baseline method is suited to a term containing a single type of character such as alphabetical words and kanji words, whereas the proposed method is suited to a term containing multiple types of character. In the future, we will apply the proposed method to Japanese abbreviations generated with transliteration between English and Japanese[17]. We also plan to narrow down the top ranked abbreviation candidates by using the search results on the Web.

References

Eytan Adar. 2004. SaRAD: A Simple and Robust Abbreviation Dictionary. *Bioinformatics*, 20(4):527–533.

Masanori Enoki, Mika Koho, Kenko Ota, and Masuzo Yanagida. 2007. Automatic Generation Abbriviated Forms of Japanese Expressions and its Appritions to Speech Recognition (in Japanese). *IPSJ SIG Notes*, 313–318.

[17]For example, "ミュージックステーション (music station)" is abbreviated as "M ステ (emu sute)". It is created by using a substring "M" of "Music" translated from "ミュージック" and a substring "ステ" of "ステーション".

Toru Hisamitsu and Yoshiki Niwa. 2001. Extracting useful terms from parenthetical expression by combining simple rules and statistical measures: A comparative evaluation of bigram statistics. Didier Bourigault and Christian Jacquemin and Marie-Claude L'Homme editors. *Recent Advances in Computational Terminology*, 209–224.

John Lafferty, Andrew McCallum, and Fernando Pereira. 2001. Conditional Random Fields: Probabilistic Models for Segmenting and Labeling Sequence Data. *Proceedings of the ICML-2001*, 282–289.

Christopher D. Manning and Hinrich Schutze. 1999. The MIT Press. *Foundations of statistical natural language processing*.

Norifumi Murayama and Manabu Okumura. 2006. Automatic Generation of Abbreviations with Noisy-channel model (in Japanese). *NLP2006*, 763–766.

Norifumi Murayama and Manabu Okumura. 2008. Statistical Model for Japanese Abbreviations. *Proceedings of the PRICAI-08*, 260–272.

David Nadeau and Peter D. Turney. 2005. A supervised learning approach to acronym identification. *Proceedings of the AI'2005*, 10 pages.

Naoaki Okazaki and Sophia Ananiadou. 2006. Building an abbreviation dictionary using a term recognition approach. *Bioinformatics*, 22(24):3089–3095.

Naoaki Okazaki, Sophia Ananiadou, and Jun'ichi Tsujii. 2008(1). A Discriminative Alignment Model for Abbreviation Recognition. *Proceedings of the Coling 2008*, 657–664.

Naoaki Okazaki, Mitsuru Ishizuka, and Jun'ichi Tsujii. 2008(2). A Discriminative Approach to Japanese Abbreviation Extraction. *Proceedings of the IJCNLP 2008*, 889–894.

Youngja Park and Roy J. Byrd. 2001. Hybrid Text Mining for Finding Abbreviations and Their Definitions. *Proceedings of the EMNLP-2001*, 126–133.

Masahiro Saikou, Kiyokazu Miki, and Hiroaki Hattori. 2008. Automatic Generation of Abbreviations with Probabilistic Models (in Japanese). *The Acoustical Society of Japan*, 237–238.

Hiroyuki Sakai and Shigeru Masuyama. 2005. Improvement of the Method for Acquiring Knowledge from a Single Corpus on Correspondences between Abbreviations and Their Original words (in Japanese). *Journal of Natural Language Processing*, 12(4):207–231.

Ariel S. Schwartz and Marti A. Hearst. 2003. A Simple Algorithm for Identifying Abbreviation Definitions in Biomedical Text. *Proceedings of the PSB-2003*, 451–462.

	Case A	%	Case B	%	Total
Alpha	917	(98.8)	11	(1.2)	928
Kata.	0	(0)	245	(100)	245
Kanji	363	(91.0)	36	(9.0)	399
Univ.	513	(98.1)	10	(1.9)	523
TV1	27	(8.3)	299	(91.7)	326
TV2	49	(8.1)	554	(91.9)	603
Total	1869	(61.8)	1155	(38.2)	3024
(Rec@30)					
CRF	-		-		87.0%
CRF/LLM	97.1%		76.9%		89.4%

Table 5: The number of abbreviations in case A and B for the six data sets, and recall in the top 30.

< Alphabetical Words >

	Abbr.
Japan Electronics and Information Technology Industries Ass	JEITA
Nippon Telephone and Telegraph corporation	NTT
Freedom Of Mobile multimedia Access	FOMA

< Katakana Words >

	Abbr.
オートマチックトランスミッション (Ootomachikku toransumissh (automatic transmission)	オートマ(Ootoma)
スーパーコンピューター (Suupaa conpyuutaa) (super computer)	スパコン(Supa con)
アメリカンフットボール (American futto booru) (American football)	アメフト (Ame futo)

< Kanji Words >

	Abbr.
私的独占の禁止及び公正取引の確保に関する法律 (Shiteki dokusen no kinshi oyobi kousei torihiki no kakuho ni kansuru houritsu) (Act on Prohibition of Private Monopolization and Maintenance of Fair Trade)	独禁法(Dokkin hou)
全日本民主医療機関連合会 (Zen nihon minshu iryou kikan reng (Japan Federation of Democratic Medical Institutions)	民医連(Miniren)
大学入学資格検定 (Daigaku nyuugaku sikaku kentei) (the University Entrance Qualification Examination)	大検(Dai ken)

< Name of University >

	Abbr.
日本医科大学 (Nihon ika daigaku) (Nippon Medical School)	日医大(Nichiidai), 日医(Nichii)
名古屋商科大学 (Nagoya shouka daigaku) (Nagoya University of Commerce & Business)	名商大(Meishoudai), 名商(Meishou)
お茶の水女子大学 (Ochanomizu jyoshi daigaku) (Ochanomizu University)	お茶女(Ochajyo), お茶大(Ochadai)

< Name of TV prog. 1 >

	Abbr.
朝はビタミン (Asa wa bitamin)	朝ビタ(Asa bita)
ダウンタウンのガキの使いやあらへんで (Downtown no gaki no tsukai ya arahen de) (Downtown's "I'm Not An Errand Boy!")	ガキ使(Gaki tsuka), ガキ使い(Gaki tsu ガキ(Gaki), ガキの使い(Gaki no tsuka
水曜どうでしょう (Suiyou doudeshou) (How do you like Wednesday?)	どうでしょう(Doudeshou), 水どう(Sui d

< Name of TV prog. 2 >

おしゃれ工房 (Oshare koubou) (A nifty craft center)	おしゃれ(Oshare)
テレ遊びパフォー漫才虎の穴 (Tere asobi pafoo manzai torano	テレ遊びパフォー(Tere asobi pafoo)
3か月トピック英会話 (San-kagetsu topikku eikaiwa) (An English conversation program focusing on one theme per every three months)	トピ英(Topi ei)

Figure 2: Example of data sets.

Author Index